# THE
# SECRET
## OF LOVE

*This practical, uplifting book presents real client stories representing the whole array of relationship situations, and how clients found their own answers, rediscovered the feeling of love, and changed their lives as they came to understand the Principles behind life. The authors provide succinct and helpful commentary, but the client stories carry the message, inspiring readers to see the ordinary, yet remarkable, impact of realizing the simplicity of reconnecting to our spiritual nature and the power of thought. This is a book that will help people see beyond the mystery of seemingly intractable relationship problems. It will help counselors recognize the power of working with the health and resilience of their clients to allow clients to discover and express their own wisdom. The authors, whose own lives and work were profoundly impacted by their exposure to the Principles, are experienced and clear teachers of the Principles, and their explanations of client stories are deep and helpful. But one leaves the book being most touched by the sheer joy they share in the privilege of awakening hope, love, and a whole new vision in their clients.*

–JUDITH A SEDGEMAN, EdD,
SEDGEMAN CONSULTING LLC

# THE

# SECRET
## OF LOVE

### UNLOCK THE MYSTERY, UNLEASH THE MAGIC

**LORI CARPENOS • CHRISTINE HEATH**

Foreword by Dr. George Pransky, PhD

Three Principles Publishing

The Publisher: Three Principles Publishing is an imprint of Dragon Hill Publishing Ltd.
Website: www.dragonhillpublishing.com

**Library and Archives Canada Cataloguing in Publication**

Carpenos, Lori, author

The secret of love / Lori Carpenos & Christine Heath.—1st edition.

Issued in print and electronic formats.

ISBN 978-1-896124-70-4 (softcover).—ISBN 978-1-896124-71-1 (EPUB)


1. Self-actualization (Psychology). 2. Love. 3. Intimacy (Psychology).
4. Couples. 5. Spirituality. I. Heath, Christine J., author II. Title.

BF637.S4C379 2018          158          C2017-907494-6
                                        C2017-907495-4


*Project Director:* Marina Michaelides
*Production & Layout:* Gregory Brown
*Cover Design:* Gregory Brown
*Cover Image:* Bhavesh1988/Thinkstock

Produced with the assistance of the Government
of Alberta.

PC: 38

# Contents

# Dedication

*We dedicate this book to the late Sydney Banks. We will be forever grateful to him for sharing his insight and helping us both change and experience the magic of life.*

*He dedicated his life to ease the suffering of humanity and raise the level of consciousness of the world. We hope that this book will help people awaken to the power of love and understanding to further his mission.*

# Foreword

I have known Christine Heath as a colleague for 30 years and Lori Carpenos almost as long. They asked me to read their manuscript because I had a particular interest and background in relationships. I am the author of *The Relationship Handbook* and, for forty years, a licensed marriage and family counselor.

To say the least, I was very impressed with their manuscript and told them I would be willing to write a foreword. Here is my take on why the book is of great value to the reader.

If you randomly pick a relationship book off the shelf, you will find some or all the following topics: a discussion of compatibility, communication methodology, how to improve the dynamic of your relationship and how to deal with the most common relationship issues. If you took 5 to 10 more relationship books off the shelf, you would find the same content with different solutions to these issues.

Surprisingly, you won't find in this book any of the kind of content in most relationship books! It is for that reason that this book will be particularly impactful and useful. Let me explain. All the topics that I mentioned above do not take into account the current psychological functioning/level of well-being of the participants. All the ideas and techniques in other books are meant to improve relationships. The problem is this: participants who remain "such as they are" will be the source of their future problems. What sense does it make to take each partner's psychological functioning as a given? Wouldn't it be better to improve their functioning so that the relationship problems are minimized in the first place? This book does that very thing. In addition, Lori and Christine will show you how to take in stride whatever shortcomings may remain.

The fundamental premise is: What goes on in the minds of the participants will determine the quality of that relationship. Imagine, if you will, that what goes on in the minds of the participants is a film clip, and the quality of their day-to-day relationship is what is projected onto the screen.

The book spells out principles that will actually and significantly improve the functioning of the reader simply by understanding these simple yet powerful principles. Such a concept may seem too good to be true, but I have seen in more than 40 years of working with clients and groups how the understanding of these principles has taken people's psychological functioning to a higher level. And I will say that Chris and Lori have done a particularly good job getting across these understandings.

Bottom line: A key to relationship success lies in gracefully relating to each other's frailties. Unfortunately, or fortunately (depending on your perspective), each person has to deal with the frailties of others in their own way, within their own mind. The principles presented in this book will not only reduce the frailties of the participants, but they will also give the reader a platform for gracefully relating to the frailties of other people as they go forward. In other words, the understandings you gain from this book will naturally make you a nicer person and make you less affected, less bothered by the troublesome behaviors of others. Together those two benefits make for successful relationships. Forty years of working with couples and families have made that finding abundantly clear to me.

But this book does more than just get across an understanding of the principles to help couples and individuals. This book is more than a conceptual, theoretical work. The authors constructed this book to show you from all angles how understanding these Three Universal Principles of Mind, Consciousness and Thought play out in a myriad of relationship situations. They have assembled contributing authors who share the following characteristics:

- They are all familiar with the principles behind this book. To a person, these principles have been the foundation of their lives and relationships.
- They all face the same situations, the same issues, as the average bear. They live in the "real" world, not some fantasy existence.
- In every case, the adversity they have faced in their relationships has served to strengthen their bond and bring them closer together. The issues of growing apart or growing tired of each other have not been issues for any of them.

- Each of the couples would say that their relationship had a similar before and a similar after. Before they had these understandings, the relationship took a toll on them, in many cases, to the point of considering separation. The after relationship was so solid that they took for granted a graceful relationship existence even as they continued to face adversity.

Each of these individuals spells out chapter and verse their relationship story, warts and all. They relate what it was like and what they were up against when they struggled as a couple. They tell the story of their turnaround and, most importantly, the specific understandings that accounted for that turnaround. Lastly, each explains how it was possible that even though they faced the same issues after the turnaround, that adversity actually made them stronger as a couple rather than weaker.

As I write these paragraphs, I realize that what I'm saying might look too simplistic, too good to be true. I'm confident that won't be the case, but of course, you will be the judge. I would be very surprised, if not shocked, that any reader of this book would say, "it didn't help my relationship significantly."

If you interviewed 50 couples that struggled and 50 couples with successful relationships, you would see common themes, common understandings. You would see the same kinds of circumstances and difficulties in all one hundred relationships, but the understandings they have about how the mind works and about how relationships keep the successful couples on solid ground. The couples without these understandings about how the mind works and relationships are hard-pressed to stay on solid ground even if they love each other and try their best. Those common understandings are in this book, both in the explanations and in the stories.

I feel this book will help individuals, but more importantly, it has implications that will change the fields of psychology, and marriage and family therapy.

–Dr. George Pransky, PhD
AUTHOR OF *The Relationship Handbook*

# Authors' Preface

This book began as a compilation of amazing stories from couples whose relationships improved and, in some cases, totally turned around just by virtue of being pointed within, toward their true nature. As they gained insights while discovering the Principles discussed in this book, these couples began to see how they had been innocently contributing to their own problems. Some insights set off instantaneous shifts, others changed over time; all were positive, healthy shifts that resulted naturally from understanding the mystery behind what guides us. These couples saw how they can work with the force of nature rather than against it.

Our inspiration for writing this book came from an audiotape called "Thought and Marriage" by the late Sydney Banks. Mr. Banks uncovered the Three Principles that create everyone's experience of life. These Principles transformed how we help people. This tape exudes so much love and understanding that we would each get deeply touched no matter how many times we listened to it.

We were incredibly fortunate to have been students of Sydney Banks. It didn't take long for either of us to realize the profundity of what he was saying. At that point, the quality of our lives began to change.

We've been able to share the logic of these Principles with everyone we've come in contact with in our field of Marriage and Family Therapy, as well as in our own lives. It's been an incredible blessing, one we don't take lightly. We each know how difficult our lives could have (and probably would have) been had we not miraculously encountered Mr. Banks in 1981 and 1985, respectively.

Our transformations occurred through an ever-deepening understanding of how our experience of life comes through the operation of the Three Principles of Universal Mind, Universal Thought and Universal Consciousness, which bring us the ability to experience reality. The Principles prove that our experience of reality comes through us, not to us.

As we recognized the nature of these Universal Principles, the quality of our relationships improved, as did our ability to help others achieve the same. This change has happened for thousands of people around the globe. We believe the same can happen for you.

As you read this book, it is important that you recognize the simplicity of what we're describing. If it seems complicated, please put it down for a while, and when you come back to it look for the simplicity. It's very simple, but simplicity can be missed when the intellect tries to analyze, judge and compare things.

Each chapter consists of three parts:

1. A quote by the late Mr. Sydney Banks.

Each quote is followed by a true story, either from a recorded interview or written up from client notes (all client names have been changed), colleagues who contributed their personal stories and our own personal stories.

2. Each story is followed by the authors' reflections.

You will see what understanding these Three Principles holds for humanity. That understanding will come from you—not from us, not from Syd Banks, not from anyone or anything outside of yourself. As you uncover this deeper wisdom, your level of consciousness may rise and then your relationships will improve effortlessly.

That is our purpose in writing this book. We hope you will see the impact that an understanding of these simple Principles can have on humanity. We believe that as these Principles are realized, people will relate to one another through love and understanding. The world will change. Miracles can happen…

# Acknowledgments

We can't even begin to tell you how grateful we are to Dr. George Pransky, PhD, first for his recognition that Sydney Banks' discovery of the Three Principles had profound ramifications for the fields of psychology and marriage and family therapy. Additionally, his unwavering faith in humanity and his courage to talk about something that was a truly new paradigm in our understanding of mental well-being. He was the first therapist to rigorously formulate ideas to train anyone in the helping professions, via the Three Principles. He forged the way for countless mental health practitioners around the globe to reach their clients in ways they had never imagined possible. Furthermore, he wrote the first book for relationships, *The Relationship Handbook*, based on his understanding of the Principles. We felt honored that he would take the time to meticulously read and ensure that every sentence of our book remained true to the Principles, as he saw that this book will help people long after we are all gone. His mentorship was invaluable and pushed both of us beyond what we thought we already knew. Dr. Pransky is an amazing therapist as well as a brilliant visionary. We feel so lucky to have had the opportunity to learn from and to work with him.

We are immensely grateful to Dr. Judith Sedgeman, EdD, for her vision to expand the scope of our initial stories to include the stories of people who were really suffering in life. We knew immediately that she was absolutely correct because we'd both had experiences where understanding The Principles helped people in extremely difficult situations find a safer, healthier existence. We would not have broadened the scope without her vision. As an award-winning, renowned editor, who helped us communicate in ways that were simple yet touching, Dr. Sedgeman's encouragement throughout the project kept us going when we thought we were on our last nerve. She reminded us how much the world needed a book like this. Her brilliance, positive attitude and deep understanding of how to live in a beautiful feeling were powerful reminders throughout the evolution of this book.

Judith Sedgeman is one of the most humble people on the planet, and she has quietly done a tremendous amount of work to further the understanding of the Principles in the world.

In the beginning, when Sydney Banks first had his experience, many people learned to live in love with one another. Many of these people shared their stories for us to include in this book. We are honored that they would take the time to share something very personal in the effort to help all who would read about their experience. These couples are some of the most beautiful people in the world, and their relationships are still magical, forty or more years later. We cannot thank you enough for your generosity and continued commitment to helping others see what you found, and realizing that if you could learn how to live in this incredible reality that others could, too. Your stories made the book come to life. We couldn't have done that without you.

We want to thank our clients who agreed to contribute their stories and gave us the honor of helping them discover their innate health and wisdom. Even if your name or details were changed, you know who you are.

We both wish to thank Sam Po'omaihealani for giving up his weekends with Christine so we could work on this book. With Sam and Chris living in Hawaii and Lori living in Connecticut, the time difference was particularly challenging. Thank you, Sam; you are an absolute love! A huge thank you to Jack Pransky, PhD; Michael Neill; and Garrett Kramer for teaching us what writing and publishing a book really entails.

Thank you to Suzanne Rabus, Debbie Waterman, and Faye Boer for your technical assistance and patience. You are all angels and incredible editors.

Last, but not least, thank you Shane Kennedy for telling us that you were carrying the manuscript around with you and reading it whenever you had the chance because you loved it so much. Thank you also for your vision and dedication to keeping Sydney Banks' message alive through books, CDs and DVDs. Because of you, anyone can hear his voice or see him speak about what he found. These have been incredible resources for countless people, and they will continue to facilitate change throughout the world and be available to help people forever.

# From the Authors

## Lori

This book would never have evolved the way it did without Christine's help. It began with a compilation of stories I wrote up because I was so astonished when my clients would come in after just a few sessions with stories of the insights they were having and how their relationship was changing. I was dumbfounded since I knew the changes had nothing to do with me. I was merely pointing them to their individual innate health and wisdom. As my file of stories grew, I realized I had enough to fill a book, but writing a book was more than I was prepared to take on alone. Christine Heath immediately came to mind although we had only met in passing in 1985. She was in the outgoing class at the Advanced Human Studies Institute in Florida, and I was coming in for the next class. I remember thinking how brave she was to move from her home in Minnesota to Hawaii. She knew no one except the three therapists who went with her to start a Three Principles based mental health center. In the early years of our conferences, whenever Chris got to the podium to speak, she would start to cry; it became a joke we would tease her about. She had such a beautiful feeling about her, and I remembered her laugh. I was so pleased when she agreed to write this book with me. She sent me a cassette tape (that proves the era we began in) that Sydney Banks had made called, "Thought and Marriage." It was my turn to cry; the feeling in that tape was so beautiful. Well, the rest is history because that one tape guided this project from that point onward. I had a wonderful time working with Chris. We shared an online platform where we could see each other and the document at the same time. It wasn't all work. We laughed and told our own stories to one another, and I even got to meet her dogs! I consider her my soul sister. Now, as I write this,

I realize we formed a bond with one another while writing about relationships. How great is that? I know I will miss working on a project with Chris. It was definitely a life-altering experience and one I will always cherish.

## Christine

I am shocked and amazed that Lori got us to the finish line with this book. I would never have written this book on my own. She came to me with the idea that we collaborate to write a book that would help people to deal with each other from love and understanding instead of fear and anger. I said, "Sure, I'll help you!" I thought it would take a couple of months. So five years later, we did it! I am eternally grateful to her for asking me and putting up with my relentless review and my schedule. As I live in Hawaii and she in Connecticut (five time zones away), finding time in our days to write was a challenge. We both had to become much more rigorous (which is no small task) as we wanted this book to stand on its own, beyond our lives so that it would become something for people to go to in order to find out about the magical power of love. I know that I was challenged by my awareness of the subtleties of language in order to convey an understanding of the formless nature of life. I had to look deeper and wake up again to the power of Thought. I saw wisdom in a very new way! The wonderful nature of this work is that it continues to evolve as we evolve. How exciting is that!

The other thing we did that was interesting is that we did everything together. We wrote the entire book sitting together, 5000 miles apart, over five years, and we had no conflicts! That in itself is amazing, and the proof that what we are pointing to in this book is something we live everyday and not just something we write about!

Mahalo, Lori for listening to your wisdom and giving birth to this book, and then for trusting me to help you make it something that will really help keep people from suffering needlessly.

## Section 1

# Hope for Every Relationship

*The only problem in any relationship is negative thought.*
—SYDNEY BANKS

**Elsie:** I doubt we would still be married today if Syd Banks had not discovered the Principles in 1973. Our relationship is better today than it's ever been.

**Ken:** That's absolutely true, and we've been together fifty years!

## Chapter 1

# Change Your Self, Change Your Relationship

*Love is a feeling that comes from the energy of all things,*
*from the creation of all life.*
*The feeling already exists within us, it is who we are.*
*Love is a positive feeling.*

–Sydney Banks

## Chip and Jan

**Chip:** Our marriage was really great for the first two or three years. After two or three years of being happy, I just couldn't help but go back to my depression, anger and aggressiveness. I came from a dysfunctional alcoholic environment, which seemed to be the source of my unhappiness. My low moods started to weigh on our marriage. After six or seven years we were in really bad shape. Our marriage was pretty much over when Jan met Syd Banks.

**Jan:** I assumed that Chip's deep state of depression was because of his childhood. At the time, we had a young son who was three years old and I, too, was having a really hard time of it. I was unhappy most days. It was seldom that I actually felt happy. I was putting so much pressure on myself to be a good mom and a good wife. I thought I was totally failing at both of those things. When Chip was unhappy, I was unhappy. I felt really hopeless and insecure. I remember thinking, "I wish I could just be happy."

**Chip:** We began to hear about somebody named Sydney Banks. Friends and neighbors were starting to go to his talks, but this did not appeal to us at all because we saw these friends become happy. We thought it was ridiculous and irresponsible to be so happy-go-lucky, so we did not want anything to do with listening to somebody who was just making people happy. [*laughs*]

**Jan:** It just happened that I was with some friends of ours when they were going to see Syd. As they were my ride, I decided to go with them. I remember first walking into the house, this really beautiful quaint little house on Salt Spring Island. I first met Barb, Syd's wife at the time, who was a gentle, welcoming person. She took me into the living room, and before I was even introduced to Syd, I knew that it had to be him. He looked over, and I saw this gentle, warm person, and even though he did not fit my description of a spiritually enlightened person, I just instantly felt this beautiful feeling.

After some lighthearted conversation, the room became quiet, and Syd started to talk. I remember that, as he spoke, I felt more and more peaceful. I just let down my guard and thought, *How could this person know anything, he isn't from India, Tibet, or you know, some other faraway place, and he looks so ordinary.* In spite of that, I started to open up to what he was saying, and then it dawned on me that everything, every statement he was saying felt like pure truth. I seemed to be checking off a list in my head saying, *Yes, that is true; that is true.* I felt that I was hearing the essence of all the wise teachers since the beginning of time. I had always been intrigued by the fact that these teachers seemed to agree that we have to look within to find the answers to life. As I listened to Syd, something amazing happened. I realized that the wisdom I was hearing was not coming from this man; it was coming from somewhere inside me!

At this point, Syd looked over and caught my eye and said, "If you could see who you really are on the inside and see all the beauty and goodness that lies within you, you would have all the happiness you could ever want." I can still remember the feeling of joy and relief I felt upon hearing these words. At that point, it was as if I could see my whole life spread out before me like a beautiful pathway. I couldn't see any details of how it would look; I just knew my life was going to be fine, including my marriage.

A few minutes later, Syd changed what he was talking about, and he said, "If you ever find yourself in an argument with someone, especially with your spouse, my advice is to just let go of your side of the argument and give up trying to defend your point of view. If you can find a way to take your mind off it and stop talking about it, you will find this really helpful." This was a new concept for me. Chip and I were constantly arguing. I had always thought that whenever I was in an argument with Chip, it was important for me to win because I was usually right! [Laughs] It seemed like we could never agree on anything. It was rare that we would just be in a nice feeling. He would try to defend what he saw, and I'd try to defend the way I saw it. But as I listened to Syd's advice on the matter, I realized that, since he was sharing so much wisdom, maybe I should give these suggestions a try.

I had never felt so at peace in my life as I did that day, listening to Syd talk about the spiritual side of life. Later in the day, after a long journey home with our friends, I remember walking up to the house, opening the door and being so happy to see Chip; I began to tell him about my afternoon. I thought he would be thrilled as we had been searching for so long.

**Chip:** I remember Jan came in the door with this huge grin on her face, and she starts telling me this whole story, and I'm listening.… She essentially starts telling me that we really didn't have any problems. That all the stuff we are going through is really just thought. I am like, "What? Oh my God, that is so simplistic and stupid! How could you even say it?" I got really upset; I started arguing with her, and she started arguing with me. Then I saw something for the first time. Jan just stopped. And she just looked at me. And the look wasn't like aggression; it was just beautiful— as I look back on it now, a look of love. And then she just walked away. This really ticked me off! In my mind, she should've stood there and argued it out with me!

Later, as I watched her playing with our son, looking really happy, I remember my thought was, "Well, she will be back to normal in the morning. She just had some kind of temporary euphoria, listening to this guy talk."

When I woke up in the morning, I could hear singing coming from the kitchen. My thought was, "What is this? There is never singing in my house in the kitchen!" It was Jan! She was in a really great mood. She tried to tell me more about what she was seeing differently. I just would not have it.

This lasted for a couple of weeks; I began to feel more and more desperate to have Jan back where we were before. I was so lost because the pattern of our marriage, the pattern of our arguments had just suddenly been ripped out from under me, and I did not know what to do. I really wanted it back the way it was, as strange as that sounds now.

It seems to me that all people and couples have their red buttons that you should never push, things you should never talk about, things you can guarantee will set off an argument. And so I started pushing Jan's buttons. The first few times I could see her get upset, but I would always see that moment when she just pulled back and then did something that seemed ridiculous, like asking if she could fix me a cup of tea or she would just go off for a walk.

This continued until one time, she teared up and got really upset. I felt satisfied; I finally got her back to the person I knew. I'd made it happen again. But this time she stopped; she pulled herself together and offered me a cup of tea! I remember this as the loneliest time of my life because I was totally on my own. It was like we had been in this serious dance, like the tango throwing our heads back and forth, and then Jan just stopped and quietly sat down. As I kept "doing the tango" by myself it began to feel silly, but at the same time I could not stop.

**Jan:** One day I was reflecting on what Syd said: that inside of everybody is all that goodness. I happened to look over at Chip. It suddenly occurred to me, "Oh my goodness, I have been waiting for Chip to change, and he doesn't need to change! He's beautiful just the way he is." In that moment when I was looking at Chip, I saw past the anxious, intense expression on his face. It was as if he changed before my eyes, and I saw the Chip I first fell in love with; I just saw his essence. That changed the way I related to him. I could see that there wasn't anything wrong with him, regardless of his state of mind. I had begun to see the innocence in myself, and this helped me to see the innocence in my husband! I would still get frustrated about his behavior, but as soon as I calmed down, lo and behold, I began to see his behavior change.

**Chip:** One day Jan was on the floor playing with our son, Peter, and the sun was streaming in through the window. I saw the light shining on her face and on her hair. I was looking at them, and out of nowhere a deep feeling of love just welled up from within me. I remember thinking it really was just thought, and there was nothing to do but surrender to that beautiful feeling. From that day, our marriage totally changed. We went from having trouble being around each other to living with a feeling of love for each other. Being parents became a more joyful experience as well, and within a year or so our daughter Heather was born. We have our ups and downs just like everyone else but very little upset. I can honestly say that our love and our relationship have gotten better every day.

We continue to listen to and read Syd's words, and we will be forever grateful for the understanding we have found and the life that we have been given.

## *Reflection*

As you read this story you can feel that something changed within both of these people. As they each had separate insights, they changed in different ways at different times, improving the quality of their relationship. Jan's new understanding allowed her to live in a more peaceful, loving feeling, which had a positive impact on their interactions. That is why we call this chapter "Change Your Self, Change Your Relationship." The feeling this couple described is a feeling that you are looking for in your relationship, but it is really found within yourself. In fact, we have found that even if just one person in a relationship gains an understanding of how Thought creates experience and then lives in a nicer state of mind, the relationship will improve. We call this feeling many things—gratitude, mental well-being, kindness, grace, love and so on.

This state of love and well-being is a self-righting power that we're born with. It's innate. All babies return to a more peaceful, calm state of well-being once they are past their upset. We never lose that self-righting ability; we just lose track of the fact that it is always within us. We call this *innate health* in that we are born with the ability to live in a healthy state of mind. Some people naturally live in this state of mind more than others; and as a result, they usually have long, happy marriages.

The following is an example of someone who knew nothing about the Principles intellectually, yet he certainly tapped into the promise of what this understanding holds for all of us.

## Wayne

So today, May 21, is our 44th anniversary. I got to marry the most beautiful person I know on a most beautiful day. It was 3:00 PM on a Sunday afternoon that we said, "I do." It was 95 degrees that day. I never noticed as I was enchanted by the girl in white! I remember looking at my parents and then her mom, and thinking, *This is right,* as I watched her walking up the aisle on the arm of her dad. I knew I had made the right choice. My eyes became moist with happiness. We have been through a lot of ups and downs, good times, bad times, sickness and health, riches and poorness, but I always felt the Good Lord put us together for a reason. Happy Anniversary to my sweetheart, love of my life, soul mate, kindest, most loving, beautiful girl in the world. Love you Mims!!

# *Reflection*

You can hear in his story that Wayne still has deep feelings of love throughout forty-four years of marriage to the same person. Wayne posted this on Facebook, on his forty-fourth anniversary, to express his love for his wife. A long-term marriage doesn't have to get old or boring and stale; it can get deeper, and you can create an experience beyond your expectations. How lucky for Wayne that he's still in touch with these feelings of love forty-four years later.

Love is our default setting when we're not wanting it or looking for it. In fact, it's who we are at our core. There's nothing to seek, only to express what is already yours. Another way to say it is that you already are what you seek; the essence of who we are is pure Love.

When love is unleashed inside of you, you'll know that you've found what you're looking for. You can't make yourself feel that on demand; it occurs naturally and seems almost mystical when it happens. You'll shift on a spiritual level, and then you'll see life from a different vantage point. This is the inside-out nature we're pointing toward. Some people may have a huge shift, and suddenly their life changes. Even when nothing on the outside has changed, everything may look and feel different. For instance, your wife becomes the most beautiful person in the room; you unexpectedly feel gratitude for your job; you feel compassion and understanding for your husband.

Falling in love, or falling back in love, is so easy. It just happens. We don't make it happen. We couldn't, even if we tried. Most of us would agree that it's the best feeling there is. There is nothing quite like it.

Then unexpectedly, our feelings change. This can happen just as fast. We lose our good feelings, and it seems as though it's the other person's fault. After all, it appeared as though they made us feel good, so it must also be them making us feel bad.

No one can help us fall in love because the feeling comes from within. No one can give it to us, and no one can take it away. Love is our default setting. It comes from a reservoir deep within our souls that is always accessible whether we know it or not.

In a nutshell: Feeling love is easy, that is, until we contaminate the feeling with negative or insecure thinking. When people fall into a state of love, it happens with little effort. As time goes by and couples get to know one another better, they start developing thinking about their partner based on their own perceptions about them. Whether we think of their endearing qualities or annoying qualities, our perception of that person begins to change. It never occurs to us that it is our own creation, an illusion created from our personal perspective, in that moment. What we believe we "know" about the other person is what we've conjured up in our own minds, and it can easily get in the way of the natural love we once felt.

What we think about each other and ourselves will either support love or diminish love. To understand how this plays out, we have to explore the source of all emotions—Mind, Thought and Consciousness.

The Three Principles explain that your partner's words and behaviors are the result of thought that looks real in the moment. By understanding these Principles, we can see that everyone gets tricked by their thinking to a greater or lesser extent. Being aware of this fact reduces our tendency to blame or judge our partner because we realize that we're creating it. We're creating our experience.

The way to understand what is in this book is not through words; however, that is the only way we can convey something intangible—by spoken or written word. The way to understand what we're attempting to convey is through a feeling. To see what it is, we have to bypass our intellect (which wants to analyze, judge, compare and contrast), so it would be wise not to think about our words, just get the feel for what we're saying. Our words are merely a pointer to discover the truth that lies within you.

## Jonathan and Sheryl

Jonathan came to see me, distressed over his relationship with his wife, Sheryl. He told me that Sheryl had become very reactive and angry and barely spoke to him. She no longer wanted to be intimate. She would blame him for minor things and become quick to judge him. Jonathan said that she started traveling to Washington, DC, frequently, and when she traveled she almost never called home. He would call her if things happened with the children, but they would frequently go days without communicating. He felt that it must be his fault since she frequently blamed him for anything that didn't go the way she wanted. Jonathan wanted to know what was wrong with him that Sheryl had grown to dislike him so much. He also felt hopeless because she refused to attend marriage counseling and even refused to discuss it with him.

Jonathan wanted to know what he could do to make Sheryl love him again. I told him that there was nothing he could do to change or fix himself so she would love him again. If that were possible, I would be a millionaire and the world would be a different place where peace and love would be the standard for life. I did tell him that the best chance he had was to find peace and love within himself and start to take care of his own state of mind.

I told him that if he was secure, calm and positive, every interaction with her would be different, and she would have to change because his half of their habit was no longer the same.

Jonathan came in to see me regularly; he listened to tapes and read books by Syd Banks and really transformed. He became secure and confident and did not take Sheryl's negativity personally. He ignored what he could and gently set boundaries when it seemed wise to do so.

Sheryl got worse. She stayed away longer and was angrier when she was home. Then one day, she was getting ready to go on another trip, and she told him that she had been having an affair with a man in Washington, DC. She was going to make plans to move there and wanted a divorce.

He stayed strong and said that if a divorce was what she wanted and it felt right to her, he would agree. Just before she left for the airport, he thought to put a copy of *Second Chance* by Sydney Banks in her briefcase. He said goodbye and was surprised that he didn't feel as sad as he thought he would feel.

Sheryl returned five days later and told him that she had read the book on her trip to DC, ended the relationship with the man and agreed to go to counseling. She apologized to Jonathan and asked him to keep her. They came in for four more sessions and were falling back in love with each other. They stopped in a few years later after a bike ride and just wanted to let me know that they were still doing fine and were so grateful to have learned what they did to save their marriage.

## *Reflection*

You can see how change can happen when two people are touched by a deeper feeling of love. You can't change other people; however, this is another example of what can happen when even one person changes and moves in the direction of well-being. When Jonathan changed, his interactions with Sheryl became totally different, which resulted in her changing without even knowing it. When she read *Second Chance* by Sydney Banks, she had a profound shift and saw her life and her relationship totally differently. It was as if she had awoken from a dream. Jonathan could tell by how different she was when they interacted that this was a true shift in consciousness for her. He was then able to forgive her and totally drop the memories of their past experience. The two of them together were able to create the relationship of their dreams with one another out of a state of love and positivity.

Sometimes when people reunite after a bad experience such as an affair, they worry that their spouse will repeat their hurtful actions, and as a result, they live in fear and anticipation. When a human being has a true shift in their level of consciousness, their lives are different across the board. Everything about Jonathan's wife changed for the positive, and he could feel that Sheryl was different. They were able to let go of the past; they realized that she wasn't seeing clearly at the time. Knowing that a human being is innately healthy is what helps people accept that the negative behavior of the other person isn't personal, but a trick of the mind created by insecure thinking.

## Levels of Consciousness

When people shift on the inside, they have what we will be calling a "shift in their level of consciousness." This is something that happens on its own, simply by recognizing that our experience is always coming from within us. We can't think ourselves into a higher level of consciousness to make the shift happen. As we listen and *SEE* how the Principles work within us, our consciousness shifts on its own, and we begin to see life differently. We start to feel better, and suddenly our life looks better. When this happens, we respond differently; we naturally respond in ways that are more productive and loving. These are things that will happen after we have a shift, not before. An innate state of mental well-being is within everyone, and it is unaffected by the outside world.

Please don't judge yourself or others when you start to see how we all live at different levels of consciousness. We all want to live in a better state of mind, and knowing that will affect our relationships. The idea is to look for the innocence in ourselves and others because no one purposely chooses to live at a lower level of consciousness, even if they could do such a thing. We're all doing the best we can to have a better life, no matter how dysfunctional.

## Chapter 2

# The Principles Behind Your Experience

*Mind, Consciousness and Thought are the Three Principles
that enable us to acknowledge and respond to existence.
They are the basic building blocks, and it is through these
components that all psychological mysteries are unfolded.*
                                               −Sydney Banks

## Brooke

My husband, Will, was actually the inspiration for getting involved in my current line of work. After his brother's suicide, he went into a deep depression to the point where he was hearing voices in his head. It was scary for both of us. As a result, I went to a community training about the Three Principles given by The Cypress Initiative. I knew nothing about The Cypress Initiative or the Three Principles at the time. I just had this inclination to go after I saw a community presentation on the Modello project. I wanted to help Will, but to be honest the training went right over my head. However, they did talk a lot about thoughts, and I knew Will was struggling to reconcile his thoughts with himself. One night, without any planning on my part, I nonchalantly explained what I got from the training. Then I went on about my life, not giving it another thought. At the time, I didn't even understand what I was talking about. About a month later, Will told me he had stopped taking his depression meds a month earlier; so basically, right after I went to the training. I kind of grilled him about stopping cold turkey without a doctor's orders. He responded,

"You're the one who said it was just a thought." That was about three years ago now, and he's never looked back. Needless to say he got it WAY before I did.

I was just leaving my long-time job at a local non-profit when I saw the community presentation on the Modello project, and then heard they were looking for trainers. Something in me told me to reach out to The Cypress Initiative. Honestly, in my mind, it gave me something to do while I was looking for another job. The training was about three months long. Will stopped taking his medication shortly after the training began. The reason that shocks me so much is that I must've only had one training session about this understanding before I mentioned to him what I was learning. I mean, I went through the majority of the training thinking it was going over my head and yet, he heard something profound through me after one class. Wow!

I began to see how I was creating a lot of anxiety around my second grader and her success in school. I had previously self-diagnosed my daughter with OCD, and magically she began to excel in school instead of struggling. The main takeaway for me was: Be Present. Ninety-nine point nine percent of the stuff I spent my time worrying about never materialized, and I was missing out on life in the meantime. About a month later I realized that all the worry, depression and stress I once felt was gone.

To say this understanding has changed me and my family's life would be a complete understatement. I think people can get wrapped up in past circumstances and/or controlling the future. Between Will spending the majority of his time dwelling on the past and me spending my time trying to control the future, we were living in a constant state of insecurity and fear. Now we spend the majority of our time enjoying each other and our children a whole lot more. And when we aren't enjoying each other, we spend way less time taking it seriously.

# *Reflection*

Brooke's experience is a wonderful example of how we all know that we are thinkers and that we create our reality from within, through the Principles, even if we're not awake to it. Brooke simply shared what she heard, but what happened to Will came from his own wisdom, from his awakening to the health that was already inside of him. Brooke's experience was less dramatic than Will's but equally powerful. Over time she started living in a higher level of consciousness and started having insights that kept her changing and living in deeper levels of mental well-being. As the two of them changed, their daughter followed and started living in a healthier state of mind as well, and that happened without any outside influence.

## Christine

I began my career in the mid '70s as a feminist family therapist. I worked primarily with women who had been sexually or physically abused and traumatized at some point in their lives. I did not work with men simply because they were men. I had lots of negative thinking about men and generally thought that men were creatures from the Black Lagoon in terms of how they treated women and how they interacted in the world. This, of course, made it hard for me to have a relationship with a man!

When I first got hit with how the Principles worked, I was amazed at how much better I felt about everyone, especially men. I no longer saw them as the enemy, feared them or reacted to personal things they said to me.

People noticed how much I had changed, and colleagues, mostly male, came up to me and told me how they had been afraid to talk to me in the past and how much more approachable I seemed to them. I thought this was really funny because I knew that I had been extremely insecure.

Then one day I had a huge insight. I realized that men were not different from women in how they created reality. Then I thought, *Oh my, men really aren't different from women.* The Principles worked the same in everyone! I suddenly realized that all of their bad behavior was just the result of their thoughts of insecurity. I also realized that I had a tainted view of men, given the particular clientele I was working with at the time. With that insight, I knew that I could now help them. This insight came in April. By June, half of my caseload was male, and I had never told anyone about the insight or that I was available to see male clients. I just know that when I had that insight, my whole practice changed without me doing anything.

# *Reflection*

Christine's experience is another example of how things change on the outside when one has a shift in awareness of the inside-out nature of life. She didn't realize there was anything she needed to change, yet she changed across the board. When we change on the inside, the outside follows.

She first awakened to how the Principles worked within herself and then she could see how they worked in everyone. Her understanding deepened as her feelings of anger, stress and depression virtually disappeared. This is the kind of thing that can happen when one has a deep insight. True transformation can happen without effort, just by seeing how reality is created from within.

Now you can see how an insight into the way reality works will transform you. You can see that the transformation changes not only your state of mind, but your thinking and behavior as well as how you react to others. This transformation is set into motion with an insight into the Principles of Mind, Thought and Consciousness. The next section will describe these Principles. Seeing how these Principles work can create change within yourself and your partner. Remember: Look for simplicity.

## *The Three Principles*

The word "principle" describes a phenomenon that exists whether we know about it or not. Similar to the principle of gravity, the Three Principles behind the human condition exist within every person, although most people are unaware. Gravity always existed, even before its discovery. The principle or law of gravity became the means to describe the invisible force that attracts matter toward the center of the earth.

The principle of gravity describes a universal (true everywhere on our planet) *physical* law that is constant. The Three Principles we refer to describe a universal (true for all people everywhere on the planet) *spiritual* law. They describe how the psyche and spirit come together to give us an experience of life, constantly. We can count on them to work within us, and within everyone else, always. They are the means to describe the invisible force behind human behavior.

Sydney Banks discovered these Principles in 1973. The Principles have provided a new paradigm for improved relationships. They explain how reality is created for each one of us. He explained them as follows:

### Mind
Universal Mind is the intelligence of all things, whether in form or formless.

### Consciousness
Universal Consciousness is a gift that enables us to observe and experience the existence and the workings of the world we live in.

### Thought
Universal Thought is also a gift that allows us to think our way through this cosmic drama.

> *All Three Principles are spiritual by nature and therefore have no form. That is why all three are intangible—indefinable in intellectual terms—and hence need to be expressed metaphorically.*
>
> –SYDNEY BANKS

Getting the feel for living from the understanding of how the energy of life plays out through us is like learning to ride a bicycle. You think you can just get on and ride, but you quickly realize there is a trick to staying upright. As you try to ride, you realize the trick is to click into the feeling of balance on the bicycle. Once you do that, you may be wobbly, but eventually you can ride with no hands! This is like the power of seeing how our experience is created at a deeper level than our intellect. The Principles help us see how our psychological balance works so we can better maneuver the path of life we are on. But remember that the Principles are not things or pieces of information to intellectually understand and apply, rather a description of the ability to create a reality. Listening to the feeling of psychological balance and looking in the right direction helps us become better "life riders," and better overall at the game of life.

Try to remember that you are not "doing the Principles." They are not things to do or not do. They are simple words that describe the way the energy of life comes through us. You can't get it or lose it because you are it. You are the energy of life, and the Principles are gifts that create our reality. They simply help us understand how things work so we can maneuver through life with more grace, happiness and joy. So, in essence, we are what we are looking for! We just have to look inside and see that life is a magical trip that is created moment to moment. Look for a feeling…It's all about the feel of balance in life.

The value in becoming aware of the Three Principles is that you can navigate through life more easily and more efficiently when you understand how it all works. These Principles are simple, yet extraordinarily profound.

*Man cannot make principles; he can only discover them.*
–Thomas Paine, *The Age of Reason* 1794, 1795, 1807

As people gain an understanding of how the Three Principles work together, they find it easier to navigate life's ups and downs, and they have a better understanding of others—which in turn, alleviates many disagreements and upsets. When you and your partner understand the Principles, you will work better together, with greater respect and ease.

Sydney Banks often referred to them as "Divine Principles" because of their spiritual nature. They are formless. They refer to the source of everything, encompassing everything in the natural world as well as everything within the psyche and spirit of individuals. They are the building blocks that bring formless energy into the world of form. By seeing how they operate within us, we realize our capacity to regulate our experience of life more optimally.

> ...we have to recognize that we are spiritual beings with
> souls existing in a spiritual world as well as material beings
> with bodies and brains existing in a material world.
> –SIR JOHN C. ECCLES (1903–97)

Please don't try to understand this intellectually. Don't get caught up in the words. The words can only be used as pointers to what you see for yourself. The idea is for you to get the feel for how you operate within yourself. It is amazing what happens when you take the focus off your partner and what they are doing, or not doing, and look within yourself instead. The Principles explain this inside-out nature of experience.

The Principles of Mind, Thought and Consciousness are a constant force of nature that work through us to create all human experiences. They explain why your partner can appear as a blessing on one day and a curse the next.

We all know *that* we think, but we really can't understand the *nature* of thought by thinking about it. To understand it, you have to look deeper where you *SEE* beyond the content of your thoughts to the *power* that brings you the content.

The deeper a person understands how the Principles work, the more they see how to work with them to benefit and expand their life, rather than work against them and live a stressful life. It happens automatically; nothing could be easier. All that is necessary is a healthy curiosity about how the Principles work within you and within everyone.

We've each been touched by these Principles for more than thirty years, yet we continue to see deeper into the role the Principles play in our lives. We speak from experience—the experience of feeling both whipped around by our own thoughts and the experience of greater calm once we gained an understanding of the Principles. It's like living in two different worlds.

> *The Principles show that what we call reality is nothing more than a person's personal ideas (thoughts) of what's real and true. The Principle of Thought gives us the ability to create thoughts, which is constant within everyone. The Principle of Consciousness is your ability to be aware; it is what makes your thinking appear real and absolute, and creates your feeling of life. The Principle of Mind is the power behind it all; it powers the entire experience. Even though we describe them separately, they work as one power, and they are constant within everyone all the time. However, what we think, the content of our thoughts varies. In other words, reality is not stagnant; its appearance varies from person to person and moment to moment.*
>
> —Sharon Lowrie, MD

## Chapter 3

# Wisdom: Your Internal Compass on the Road to Change

*When the wise tell us to look within, they are directing*
*us beyond intellectual analysis of personal thought, to*
*a higher order of knowledge called wisdom.*

*Wisdom is an innate intelligence everyone possesses deep*
*within their souls, before the contamination of the outer*
*world of creation. Find the spiritual wisdom that will guide*
*you through life from within. This is where you will find*
*the feelings of love, understanding and contentment.*

–SYDNEY BANKS

## Coizie and Dicken

**Coizie:** There came a time when we faced the biggest decision of our married life together. Dicken was offered a position in the Pacific Northwest, but we were living on the east coast and our son was still in high school.

We started to have conversations about moving and immediately one or two or all three of us would just start having upset thinking, and we would get scared, or I would cry. It seemed like we didn't know what to do or what could possibly be the solution. So when we began trying to figure out how we were going to work this out, we all agreed that we would only talk about it when we were all in pretty good states of mind. And if any of us got upset while we were talking, we would stop. We knew that at some point we would come to agreement. We trusted that would happen. But it wouldn't happen if we were upset and having a hard time talking about it, so we started and stopped the conversation several different times over the next few weeks.

Then one time, one of us had a different idea—a completely new thought that none of us had even considered—which was for Dicken to go out to Washington by himself, and I would stay back with Ben until he finished his last year of high school. It made so much sense to all of us immediately. It was a big relief, and it felt so right that we just trusted it.

Immediately, we began to put our energy into thinking about what we could do to make it the absolute best year that our family ever had. We all began to get creative and came up with new ideas for how to do that, and it ended up creating a remarkable growth-filled year for all of us. I don't think we would have gotten there if we had used our old way of thinking. We probably would have forced a decision that would have been really difficult for somebody. Most likely, we would have forced our son to move with us.

**Dicken:** That is just one example of how, by learning the Principles, we began to trust in our own wisdom. We learned that the answers would be there when we were in mental clarity as opposed to when we were anxiety-ridden. Our understanding of the Principles allowed us to trust our wisdom.

## *Reflection*

You'll notice in this story, as in many of the stories in this book, the family was able to navigate discussions according to the feeling and state of mind of each individual within the group. They also knew they could trust that wisdom would help them see the best solution that would work for everyone.

Wisdom is the ability to recognize our own thinking and see it for what it is. It also allows us to recognize that we are part of the spiritual energy of life. Wisdom is the space we come from when we have clear thinking, and we can navigate through life more optimally. Wisdom is an internal intelligence that comes to us from Mind. How wisdom manifests in our life is what we call clear thinking, a feeling of knowing or intuition. Wisdom is a transcendent intelligence from which we're able to see the best answer possible for that particular situation. Wisdom may not always tell you exactly what to do in your life, but this state of mind will help you recognize the best answers possible at the time. These answers will be good for everyone, not just you.

Wisdom is impersonal and always directs us to the common good. Wisdom is never selfish, careless or dangerous. When we disagree with people or see things differently, wisdom will help people arrive at alternatives that will work for everyone as in the case of Coizie and Dicken's story. When we are caught up in our thinking, we can only see the answer we've already come up with, blinding us from the ability to come up with a whole new answer. When we understand how wisdom works, we're less attached to our own ideas because we know there is always another answer. We just have to wait for it to appear. Knowing there is another answer makes life less scary, and we feel more confident because we know that eventually we'll see what to do.

Understanding that wisdom comes from our spiritual essence gives it more credibility. So then we pay more attention to it because we know that we can trust that state of mind. Then it's easy to let go of the answers we've already formulated that won't fit for everyone concerned. Whether you are coordinating between individuals or in a group, the answer will feel right to everyone. When the people involved get that feeling of *yes, that's the answer,* you know that everyone is on the same page, and then everyone can get behind whatever the change is.

> *When the answers are complicated, it is the Intellect. When the answers are simple, it's the Spirit.*
>
> —SYDNEY BANKS

Frequently we are asked: How do I know that what I'm thinking is coming from wisdom? When we listen for a feeling, we can tell the difference. Wisdom always settles you down and comes with a sense of *knowing*. When we're listening to wisdom, the answers that come will be good for everyone, not just for you. For example, your decision to divorce or not would be based on what was right for everyone—your children, your spouse, not just you. Frequently, our egotistical or insecure thinking creates an illusion that our wisdom is directing us to do something because we have a good feeling or because we think it's fate. We can get tricked into doing things that turn out to be bad ideas in the long run. We all have to learn the difference between personal thoughts seeming right and wisdom feeling true. If you have to continually justify what you did, that was not coming from wisdom.

> *Let your mind be still, for the wisdom you seek is like that butterfly over yonder. If you try and catch it with your intellect, it will simply fly away. On the other hand, if you can still your mind, someday when you least expect it, it will land in the palm of your hand.*
>
> –SYDNEY BANKS

# Chapter 4

# Understanding the Thought-Feeling Connection

*Feelings are thoughts in action.*
*Feelings are a barometer of how thoughts are being utilized.*

−SYDNEY BANKS

## Coizie and Dicken

**Dicken:** After being introduced to the Principles, I began to wake up to the enormous amount of thinking I was doing and saw that I had been generating tension and stress. The more I woke up to the fact that my thinking was creating my stress, the more I began to back away from, let go of or fall away from the thinking that I was doing and saw that it was unnecessary.

From this new understanding, I naturally found myself being much less preoccupied when I was home and was more present as a result. I became less serious and more lighthearted, more playful at home and with my kids. Going from preoccupied to being more present was directly and immediately dramatic in my case. I had been so preoccupied that my kids called me a space cadet.

**Coizie:** It was a big discovery to see that our thinking creates our moods. Like everyone, the quality of our thinking went up and down. Instead of believing that what we think when we are in a low mood means something significant and should be talked about in the relationship, we began to see low-mood thinking as normal and that you didn't really have to pay attention to that thinking. It would pass pretty quickly, and boy, did that make things easier in all of our relationships.

We didn't feel compelled to have to talk about things when we were upset. We didn't take each other's low moods so personally, so it became more and more just a normal cycle and nothing to really be concerned about.

Feelings no longer were statements about the relationship. They just became indicators of the quality of thought that was coming through us. That was huge. It took the pressure off. In the past, if Dicken got into a low mood and seemed pretty serious, I would sometimes think that meant something about me, that he was mad at me or unhappy with me. So I thought that we needed to discuss it. And unfortunately, we would. [*laughs*]

To this day it is such a relief not to feel like there are issues and problems and things that we need to talk about. We just know that in a better mood, when better thinking starts coming through, it either won't be a problem or it will look different or there will be a solution that comes to mind. It is so easy.

We started to have more trust in leaving things alone until our heads cleared, when we were in a space in which it would be very easy to see our way through any difficulties or problems or challenges. We both gained greater trust in our capacity for common sense and wise thinking. We knew that we could trust our thinking when we were calm, but not at all when we were caught up in personal thinking. This was so helpful. It paid off to just wait until the wise thinking showed up rather than work so hard when it wasn't available.

## *Reflection*

Dicken and Coizie automatically improved their communication from their understanding of the Principles. They saw that when they were emotionally reactive and in a negative state of mind, it was not the right time to try to come up with solutions. They also understood that states of mind are temporary. Their communication improved greatly as a result of this new understanding.

We are always one thought away from a better experience. Knowing this has an enormous impact on every relationship. Simply knowing that this phenomenon is true for all humans tends to move us in the direction of more positive, healthy, upbeat moments. It happens automatically; we don't have to do anything other than gain an understanding of how our thinking creates a life for us. Most people don't realize they alone are creating the experience they're having moment to moment. Moods are changes in the quality of our thinking, and therefore, our state of mind. In a more insecure or stressed state of mind, people tend to say things they don't mean, and we take things others say the wrong way, which all leads to miscommunication. It looks like our partner, the stock market, the economy or even the weather is causing our bad mood. The truth is that none of that is true; we alone make it all up via our ability to create life experience through the power of Mind, Thought and Consciousness.

We imbue everything in life with our personal take on it. In other words, what we think is what we see, and then that's what we get. It plays out for everyone in the same way.

When people know this, they know not to take their thinking too seriously when stressed, and they also know not to take their partner's emotional reactivity too seriously. It's the quality of our thinking that creates what we call moods. Everyone knows what we mean by bad moods and good moods and that the quality of our thinking changes throughout the day. We are all moody to some degree because of our thoughts.

Thought and Consciousness work together to create what we call our feelings and emotions. Essentially, we walk around feeling our thoughts whether we know it or not. In fact, we can't feel anything except what is created by thought. Even our five senses are activated by the amazing gift of thought. We don't have to know what we're thinking in order to feel it.

When we are in a more secure state of mind, we feel more positive emotions, and our cup looks half full. When we are in a more insecure, reactive state of mind, our cup looks half empty, but it's still the same cup. Our feelings and emotions alert us to whether we are in a secure, healthy state of mind or we are in a more insecure, stressed state of mind.

## Ami

I love my husband a lot, he loves me a lot and we have been through a lot. I feel really grateful because I look around, and I don't see most relationships working out so well, except for a lot of people in the Three Principles community. They're not perfect either, but having an understanding of where your experience comes from every moment really brings a place of solace, a place of rest. That's what it feels like it's become for us—that there is a core of peace and love in each of us, in the relationship, that is untouched by any turbulence that may come and go. That core is untouched whether we are "together" physically or not.

I've really learned that a relationship can be imperfect, and you can go through a fight and have some rough areas, or maybe you're not so compatible in some areas, but that's also okay.

When I was younger, I used to think if we had a big fight or there was some area where we were very incompatible, that meant we shouldn't be together. It was very traumatic for me when something like a big fight would happen. And now, I just notice that we go through phases where one person will be stressed, and you know, either of us is going through something, and it doesn't have to mean a whole lot.

## On the Possibility of Divorce

I remember driving to the park once by myself and being so upset because we just had a fight (we had just had our first child, and it was a very busy, somewhat stressful time), and the thought I had was that "I can't get a divorce!" One, because my parents had gotten a divorce when I was three years old, and I vowed that I would not do the same thing. I remember the sort of trauma of that time period of my life, even at the age of three. And I think also being involved in the Three Principles community I had the extra added pressure, thinking we're not supposed to get divorced.

But then, I suddenly realized that I could get a divorce, and that was incredibly freeing. This thought came out of nowhere, that anything was possible, and whatever happened, I would be okay. It was like a weight lifted off my shoulders, and then I was able to go back to my marriage with the understanding that we could get divorced! We might get divorced, but in this moment, all that's happening is what's happening. The future did not have to feel so heavy or play so heavily into the moment.

When I allowed for the fact that anything could happen, I was able to actually avoid getting a divorce. I have learned to kind of get quiet and see where my heart really wants to be. Every time, I feel like, "Oh, my gosh, maybe we should get a divorce"; I now say, "Okay, wait a second,"…and there is never a reason to get divorced.

So my assumption now is that if we need to get divorced, it will feel like wisdom and it will feel right. That's certainly a possibility for us or for anyone…but that was not how a "fight" felt.

I had always experienced "getting a divorce" with a lot of emotions and thoughts, and I learned to not trust that thinking. The feeling state would always be so much better when I waited. I just waited until I calmed down. And then the love would come back, and the whole question of divorce would be off the table!

## Reflection

Ami's experience is an example of someone's thinking when they are in a low mood and upset. When people get upset with their partners, they can become emotionally reactive and start thinking that divorce is inevitable. Thinking about what to do when you're upset is never a good idea. The best thing to do when you start thinking like that is to calm down, like Ami did, and then you'll get an insight about what you need to do, in the moment, to get back to a state of emotional balance. Once back in balance, you'll realize you were both in a bad mood and said things you didn't really mean. This will only become a problem if you take your own emotional reactivity or your partner's reactivity as a sign of truth about your relationship. Everyone's reaction always comes from the state of mind they are in at the time; it is never a sign that the relationship is doomed.

Remember that your experience is coming from your own thinking not the outside world, no matter how much it appears to be externally activated. In other words, your partner is never to blame for how you feel—it's always an inside job. We search for someone to bring us a beautiful feeling, when in fact beautiful feelings can only come from within us.

> *Look for a beautiful feeling.*
>
> –SYDNEY BANKS

As our thinking changes, our behavior follows, all quite naturally. The deeper we understand the effect the Three Principles have on our lives, the more positive our behaviors tend to be. The reason our behaviors become more positive is because when we're in a better state of mind, we see life from a different vantage point. We see a different reality, so we respond differently. We don't have to work at changing. We will automatically react differently when we see life differently. That is how true and lasting change occurs. It is a shift in a level of consciousness. As we wake up to the fact that our thinking creates our experience, the quality of our life improves. When we're in a better state of mind, everything we think, do and say comes from a deeper feeling of love.

> *It's our thoughts, just our thoughts, that create the feeling of love.*
>
> –SYDNEY BANKS

## Kara

I can see that to whatever extent I'm living in negativity, it just means I have lost sight of my understanding of the Principles. When I was upset, I'd lost sight of the role of my thoughts and I blamed my husband for causing me upset.

It's made my relationships so much easier. It has protected me from people's shortcomings, from people's ups and downs and from my own ups and downs. I see that with all the relationships in my life. The independence that I have gained from understanding the Principles has really allowed my relationships to be easier, to be closer and to be more connected.

# *Reflection*

Kara could see that when her level of understanding shifted, she had less reactive thinking and thus started to live in more positive feelings, automatically making it easier to navigate through life. Our awareness of how the Principles create our experience fluctuates throughout the day. When we use our feelings as a guide to our interactions with others, we navigate through life more optimally. We don't feel victimized, don't get our feelings hurt, don't hold onto resentful thinking as much and have fewer problems communicating. We get along better with others, and we have more understanding and compassion for them. Basically, life improves overall and sometimes dramatically.

When we start to feel a lot of negativity for our partner and we know it's just our thinking in the moment, that awareness will stop the cycle of reactivity. There is no sense holding on to negative feelings when you know they are simply telling you about the quality of your own thoughts. Even if it seems perfectly justified in your mind, the justification is your personal thinking too! Sometimes people will think that if they hold onto their negative feelings, they'll be protected from being hurt again. That, of course, is not true. That feeling of hurt is not coming from what happened in the past. It is coming from your current thinking of what happened in the past.

*Any projection of anger/hostility toward each other will*
*only lead to a path no one wants to be on, and eventually*
*it will lead to separation and divorce, which you don't want.*
                                                    –SYDNEY BANKS

   Angry feelings toward your partner are an alert that you perceive him or her in a way that is not healthy for you. Some people say that their angry feelings motivate them in life. However, these negative emotions are simply the result of feeling your own thinking. This doesn't mean that your partner hasn't said or done something negative; it is your personalization of the negative act that creates anger in you. Anger is not meant to be used as a defense against a perceived danger. Remember, angry feelings are just your thinking being brought to life by Consciousness.

   Fearful, negative and insecure thinking creates the feelings of anger and hatred. Believing that someone is operating with motive is usually an illusion created by insecure thinking about the other person. The more insecure thinking we generate, the worse we feel. We understand that people do scary things to one another that are horrendous and seem personal. These things can only happen when there is no understanding of the Principles. When we know that love is the answer, we see anger as a signal to quiet down and take another look when we're in a better feeling.

# Section 2

# The Secret of Love

*It's all a matter of sharing, loving and caring, never intentionally hurting your partner in any way. This is what I would call love, and this alone will create a healthy marriage.*

*—Sydney Banks*

**Dicken:** I learned that intimacy was not a function of working. You can't work your way to intimacy. It was a given that when my personal thinking would quiet down, I would feel warmth and a connection and closeness with whomever was around me. I couldn't believe it was that easy. I couldn't believe that if I got out of my own way, I would feel close and connected to people around me.

# Chapter 5

# Love is a Spiritual Gift

*Our true identity is of a spiritual nature, and it is hidden
in the very depths of each living soul on earth.*

–SYDNEY BANKS

## Coizie and Dicken

**Dicken:** After my very first training in the Principles, I made a remarkable discovery. At any moment, when I just stopped working on getting somewhere in order to develop or to achieve my well-being, the most incredible experience happened. I naturally began to feel and think better, which is what I was looking for in the first place, and I didn't have to work at it. I already had it, just naturally built in. This notion that I already had perfect well-being inside and I didn't have to develop it was a huge change for me. So as I worked less on myself and had less thinking on my mind, I became more lighthearted and more present and more available. My kids noticed it, and it sure made things so much easier for Coizie and me. We got closer and closer without even trying.

**Coizie:** …and I started having so much fun. We would allow our thinking to quiet down, and then we would feel warm, connected and so close. We would just enjoy sharing quiet time together. We started seeing how easy it was to connect on a much deeper level. We couldn't believe that we discovered something so simple that could immediately help us be warmer and more loving as parents, as well as warm, loving and intimate in our marriage. What a beautiful thing to discover and then be able to share with clients and see them have the same results very quickly. To see this happen repeatedly was just unbelievable to me. It was like a dream come true.

**Dicken:** I changed from my old patterns of being preoccupied and withdrawing. Before, I would withdraw into myself, and I would turn to my books and techniques to escape inner tension. I still experience inner tension sometimes, but it doesn't mean anything anymore. It wakes me up to the fact of thought, so I fall out of that thinking easily and quickly. I now realize that there is an underlying space I experience as welcoming, warm, loving and wise. It is my home base. For me to know that this home base is always right there inside, not just in me, but also in everybody—in my family, my friends, my clients and even in strangers—has been powerful. It lets me know that even when my kids or wife are having a difficult time and struggling, inside they are already perfectly ok. This is so helpful.

To be patient with the fact that we all get caught up at times in our own thinking is good to realize. Thoughts seem real to us, and we get stuck. Knowing that we all can get caught up in our thoughts and not realize it really helped us when our kids were teenagers and now with our grandchildren. We're sharing with them about thinking and feeling and where our feelings really come from.

**Coizie:** It just takes one person to begin to live this understanding in a family, a relationship or even an organization. Dicken was the first to learn about the Principles, but it was contagious in our family. You could see it spreading from one person to another to another, and then we would each reinforce the other just by the way we were living from this understanding. Our son's wife and our young grandchildren are all learning from both of us, and that is just so neat to think that they have already become more resilient and living life with more ease and well-being.

# *Reflection*

You can see as you read this story that love comes from within us, not from other people. One of the secrets of love is that it already exists inside of us before Thought. That is why the wise have always told us to look within and to live in love. Love can only come from within each of us.

We are all born with this state of mental well-being, which is what produces the feeling of love. It is a spiritual gift that comes with the gift of life. It cannot be damaged by anything you've done, anything that was done to you or by the circumstances of your life. Everyone can live in this state of mind most of the time, regardless of their past or present. When we are in this state of mind we feel connected to others. We want to be of service to those we care for, and we feel lighthearted and peaceful. We feel love for our family and compassion for those we once thought had "done us wrong." We feel awake and alive. This is the power of love.

This state of well-being is what everyone is looking for in their relationships, work, families and so on. We just have to look within and realize that we are what we are seeking. We have to look on the inside to find these feelings. We don't have to do anything but look within and see that there's no mystery; we've just been looking in the wrong direction.

*Just point yourself in the general direction and do nothing*

–SYDNEY BANKS

## Harry and Jessica

Harry, a client, had suffered for many years from depression. He had tried all kinds of therapy to find peace and happiness. His wife, Jessica, was ready to leave him because he was so negative and uninterested in doing anything. They had heard that I did a "new" kind of therapy, and Harry agreed to have one last try.

He came in and listened but was skeptical because there were no rituals, workbooks or techniques. The only thing I asked him to do was to read *Second Chance* by Sydney Banks. The next week he came back to my office and started to cry. He gave me the book back and said, "Do you mean there is hope for *me*?" I told him, "Yes, there is hope for all of us!"

## *Reflection*

Recognizing that love comes from within us is the hope for everyone.

We all have the capacity to get over things. This ability is built into all of us, so awakening to it provides hope and faith that no one is broken. We all come from the same source of love. It is awesome to see how fast people can change when they're looking in the right direction and realize it's just Thought getting in their way. Understanding gives hope to people who have never recovered from a past trauma or who believe they are damaged or broken by their past or their lot in life. The Principles show us that there is always a new opportunity for everyone to become their true self—pure love.

Chapter 6

# The Illusory Nature of Thought

*Life, as we see it, is governed by our own thoughts.*
*The reality we live in is a direct result of our thoughts.*
*This is very powerful when you see it.*

–SYDNEY BANKS

## Cindy

Cindy was engaged to Gabe, who had two children living with him. Cindy was bothered by what she thought were irresponsible behaviors of the children, and she pointed it out to Gabe on many occasions. She was concerned that his kids were taking advantage of him and that he wasn't setting firm enough limits in order for them to become more responsible. They had frequent arguments over his kids. She was devastated when he broke up with her and had no clue that her thinking was so toxic to their relationship.

As Cindy learned about the Principles and where her experience actually originates, she had an insight that she had been thinking it was up to her to save her fiancé from his unruly children, which is what ultimately drove Gabe out the door. She realized she had made his children her business, and that he didn't want to spend his time with her worrying about his grown kids. She also realized that her negative thinking about his situation must have felt like criticism to him.

## *Reflection*

Cindy's insight held the key to change everything. She saw how she could go from feeling annoyed to feeling tenderness. That insight was freeing for her. She saw the simplicity in it.

Because our experience is coming from our own thinking, we have the free will to take our thinking seriously or let it go. When we realize negative thinking is not a sign of truth, it's easier to let it go. Then our innate health kicks in, and more positive thoughts can come forth effortlessly. It feels like magic.

As your level of understanding of the illusionary nature of thought grows deeper, your life experiences will improve. We have a built-in resilience and a default setting of calm when we're not covering it up or contaminating it with personal, negative, judgmental thinking.

Let's face it, the level of Consciousness in the world right now is pretty low, as shown by all the wars, poverty, shootings, violence and hostility. The list goes on. The way out is not masking what exists through positive thinking. When bad things happen, if you stay in the moment, you'll see how to best handle whatever is around you in that moment.

At times, negativity seems to have a magnetic force pulling at us. People have told us they had a subtle message growing up that smart people are negative because they see reality as it is, and only fools see positivity all the time. They are unrealistic. They might think, "I'd rather look at the negative so that I am pleasantly surprised if something positive happens, and then I won't be devastated if something bad happens." Or they might think, "If I'm too positive, I won't see bad things coming, and I won't be able to ward them off."

## Joan

Joan was fifty-something when she moved into the town where I had my practice. She sought help because she was unhappy and depressed about her current living situation. She felt insecure, living away from her husband in a rural community where she had no friends or places to go to meet people. She described her perception of the local people, saying, "I really don't like people who are too positive. They are not seeing the injustices in the world; they aren't paying attention to how people are being abused and mistreated or to the politics of those in power in the world. They just have rose-colored glasses on, and what they see is distorted by positive thinking. How could anyone be lighthearted, happy and at peace in life given the current state of the world? It is like they are fake and not REAL."

I laughed, and Joan looked at me angrily because she thought I was laughing at her. I assured her that I was laughing because I had thought the same exact way in the past, until I realized that my negative thinking created what I saw in the world. Joan said, "But isn't that denial?" I said, "What if they aren't faking? Maybe they see a reality different from the one that you see because they are having different thoughts and are living in a more positive state of mind?" Suddenly, she burst out laughing and said, "Oh, my goodness! I am just seeing my own negative thoughts, and I think that's what everyone sees!"

## *Reflection*

Joan was able to see how her own negative thinking was impacting the way she saw the world. A person's thinking can have a profound effect on relationships. Imagine if everyone could see that their discontent was just coming from their own thinking? We'd be out of a job!

The quality of our thinking creates the experience we have of other people. When this experience comes from insecurity or negative beliefs, it can remind us to quiet down and wait for our mind to reset. Then our thinking becomes more positive, all on its own.

## Lori

You may wonder why a single person is writing about relation-ships. Well, you're not alone; so did I! I used to be extremely embarrassed about my single status, having grown up hearing nasty-sounding words, such as "spinster" and "old maid," to describe an unmarried woman. I also grew up reading romantic stories of charming princes slaying dragons for their princesses. My self worth was inextricably linked to external circumstances, namely having a successful marriage and being a mother.

I did an awful lot of thinking about being single. Was I single because I was faulty in some way? Did I do something wrong to lead me down this path? Did I miss doing something somewhere along the line? Was I irresponsible? I felt so much shame about it because I'd been observing relationships since I was a little girl and had always assumed I would someday be a part of a lifelong partnership.

I spent many years listening to couples' stories, hearing all the things they shared together, for example, deciding which family to spend holidays with, planning anniversary celebrations or the right college for their children. None of this was a part of my world.

As I began to see how the Principles worked to create my "real-ity," I realized that these ideas about myself were simply a bunch of thoughts I had taken seriously. I realized I had made up a story and bought into it in varying degrees depending on my mood of the moment. This insight changed my experience from downtrod-den to upbeat. I had believed in a made-up story! I'd probably still be carrying around that burden, thinking I was inferior to other women with husbands and children. Please know, my change of heart didn't happen overnight. It was a gradual realization.

I thought a lot about what kind of man would be the right match for me, as though I would know what the right partner would look and feel like. My imagination was specific in terms of physical, mental and emotional characteristics. I had no clue then that this was just my made-up thinking. I was blinded by those criteria until I wrote this book, almost thirty years after I first learned of the Principles. Now I know from my experience why they are called blind spots because we are truly blind to the power of our thinking. For example, when I went out with a man who didn't meet all the requirements on my list, I couldn't wait to get back home to read a good book. At the same time, I thought there must be something I'm doing wrong to not have met the "right" person, again! I'd feel sorry for myself, and I'd think, "Why is this happening to me?"

I thought that love came from a man or children or my relatives. I didn't realize that love came from within. This may not seem like earth-shattering news, but for me it was huge. I realized my dissatisfaction did not come from others; it could only come from my own thinking.

I hadn't realized how much my life was improving while I was writing this book, until I got curious about why I was enjoying meeting men and not getting upset even when it didn't work out. My life became easier and much more carefree. I began to live my life without worrying whether I was a single person or a coupled person. It was solely dependent on what was in my own mind in any given moment. I could date when I wanted to and spend time alone in quiet solitude doing as I pleased. I felt lucky to have that kind of freedom. Rather than looking at what was lacking, I began feeling more gratitude about all the freedoms that being single gave me! Now that's true freedom—no rules to obey, just wisdom and common sense to to guide my life.

What a relief it was to shed that thinking and enjoy dates for what they were—two people sharing some personal time together. This took the work out of meeting men and then wanting to change or fix them. Instead, I focused my energy on enjoying the company of another person. The laundry list for a partner never fully disappeared. It lurked around the perimeter of my mind, but my relationship to the list changed. Now from a deeper level, I know none of those rules I made up for a partner really matter. The only thing that truly matters is the feeling. It sounded so obvious when I first heard Syd Banks say, "Love is a beautiful feeling." Now I see the simplicity and profundity of that statement.

I used to think the world was more difficult for a single person. While couples can share the workload, we single people must do everything ourselves. Now I realize that is only the case when I think it's like that. It's the same world whether coupled or single!

So now, when someone asks why I don't have a man in my life, my answer is simple: I don't know. What I do know, beyond a shadow of a doubt, is that it simply is what it is. It's no one's fault, and it's not a matter of me being abnormal. Beyond that, I can be happy no matter what my circumstances are. Now that's a transformation.

## *Reflection*

Lori realized on a deeper level that having a long-term, loving relationship has nothing to do with compatibility, shared customs, beliefs, lifestyles or a list of specific characteristics. All of her personal thinking was based on beliefs she formed as she thought about what a good relationship would be like, what a perfect mate would be and what their interactions would be like. She realized that these ideas came from her romantic imagination and were not based on anything real. Since she thought these ideas were true, she thought such criteria would be necessary to feel happy and fulfilled. Her quest became finding the guy who met her criteria rather than finding a man who wanted to live in a beautiful feeling.

Creating and maintaining a good relationship is about living from that beautiful feeling of love, a deeper love that comes from within rather than from finding "the right person." Living from the feeling of love is what creates beautiful relationships. Two people can find that feeling within themselves. Then when they come together, they create a beautiful relationship. It happens all the time, quite by accident. People can see how to maintain that beautiful feeling when they look within and stop searching.

# Chapter 7

# Positive Change From Insight

*Realization is an insight beyond the intellect.*

–SYDNEY BANKS

## Lori

I was speaking with Keith Blevens, a Three Principles psychologist, and I recall being on a rant about not being a mother and becoming too old to even consider the possibility of motherhood. The opportunity would soon be over, and it looked to me as though that meant my life would be over. At the time, it seemed to be a terrible, impending tragedy. When I finally paused to take a breath, Keith said something, but all I heard was, "So what?"

I almost fell off my chair. As I recall, my first thought was, "What do you mean, so what?!" That is an awful thing to say to someone suffering about something she has no control over.

Still upset over what I thought was an inconsiderate remark, I walked out onto the street in a huff, and the first thing I noticed was a mother and child. It was the first time in the longest while I could remember that I didn't burst into tears upon seeing a mother and her child. I actually enjoyed seeing them! Well, that blew my mind. From that moment my thinking about seeing mothers and children together became one of my most pleasurable experiences. It was like a miracle to me.

I did not talk myself into this feeling; that would never work. It had nothing to do with positive thinking. The change came about on its own, through an insight, and it rocked my world.

It occurred to me that if something that enormous could shift my world 180 degrees, then the same sort of shift could happen with anything in my life or in anyone else's life. There are no words to adequately describe what that felt like.

It wasn't Keith's words that made the difference for me. It was my insight into those words.

## *Reflection*

Lori had an insight about the nature of Thought that allowed her to see she had made up a belief about life and her personal happiness. When she was able to see that it was just a Thought, it no longer looked real, and it no longer affected her.

People tend to feel controlled by what they think about life. In this case, Lori thought she could never be happy if she didn't have children. Once she had the insight that it was just Thought and not the truth about her happiness, all that negative thinking disappeared.

Permanent change occurs through insight. Another way to explain insight is seeing something deep within yourself—a sight from within—recognizing something you already knew but didn't realize you knew.

You may be feeling hopeless right now because it doesn't seem like anything will help you fall back in love with your partner. However, if you're open enough to get an insight, you will see what has been getting in the way of feeling love for him or her.

As marriage and family therapists, we've listened to many couples. We've repeatedly heard statements such as, "I don't love him/her anymore," and we've heard the same client suddenly discover that was just negative thinking, and they really do love their partner on a deeper level. Sometimes this even happens after divorce and remarriage!

We hope this gives you hope. As you start to see where love comes from, and you start to see the function that Thought plays in your experience, you will continue to get more insights. And those insights will bring you a more beautiful feeling. Your mind will quiet; you'll be more present; and you'll start to see things in a fresh new way. That's how it works for everyone. As your consciousness rises, so does the quality of your thinking.

Falling in and out of love illustrates the fleeting nature of Thought and therefore the fleeting nature of experience. It is harder to take our thoughts seriously once we recognize their transience. The irony is that when we do not take our thoughts so seriously, they tend to disappear quicker, allowing for a better thought to emerge.

# Chapter 8

# Separate Realities: Understanding Differences

*Do you know what is really important—the difference between what is called the personal thought and the existence of thought because thought is a divine gift that allows us to experience the existence of life itself, and freedom from thought allows us to live in certain realities in our life. Somewhere there is a common denominator where all separate realities become one.*

–SYDNEY BANKS

## Susan and Henry

Two friends, Susan and Henry decided to start a business together. They were both just finding out how the Principles work and wanted to set up their business based on what they were learning. As the details were being worked out, Susan noticed that Henry's insecurity was showing up as a ridiculous amount of attention to detail. She began feeling increasingly frustrated, but since she was learning about the Principles, she recognized her frustration was coming from her own thinking even though it looked like he was causing it. She knew she needed to find a different way to look at the situation if she wanted to make their relationship work, but she just couldn't see it differently. As she became more bothered and irritated by Henry's attention to detail, Susan's frustration started to hinder their ability to work together. It occurred to Susan to call Henry's wife, Gloria, to find out how she saw her husband's obsession with details. She thought she could learn how to have a better feeling toward Henry. Here's what Gloria said in a loving tone, "Oh, I know. Isn't he cute?" Susan nearly dropped the phone in disbelief. Then another thought came to her, *Okay, maybe I could do that.* She could see him from a place of love instead of judgment. Instantly her feelings changed, and she started laughing at herself.

*Love is the absence of judgment.*

–DALAI LAMA

## Reflection

Luckily, Susan had awakened somewhat to the Principles, which allowed her to realize that the problem was not with the way Henry handled things. The problem was in her own thinking about it. Knowing how the Principles work within everyone, Susan was able to see that even though Gloria saw the same thing in Henry, she had a different experience because she didn't have negative thoughts to contaminate her feelings of love for him. Susan had judgmental thoughts about Henry's approach to things, in which she felt quite justified. Gloria saw the same pattern in Henry's behavior, but because she had such a deep feeling of love for him, she saw Henry through the eyes of endearment and wasn't bothered by it.

The Three Principles explain why you think what you think, do what you do, see what you see, feel the way you feel and why your partner often does it all differently. The Principles not only explain how we operate and how we construe reality, they also explain why we each experience things differently. This is what we call separate realities. We're each living in our own Thought-created separate reality.

## Erika and Tim

Just like most relationships, the way my husband, Tim, goes about a lot of things is very different from the way I go about things. My way of doing things always looked right, and his way looked wrong. I had to tolerate it, tolerate him and just try to have a good attitude. It seemed to me that my ideas were solid, ironclad truth. It was that way with everything, not just the big things but about the little everyday things.

For example, the way Tim loaded the dishwasher didn't make any sense to me. He'd put things in haphazardly, whereas I was raised to be as efficient as possible so you could fit the most number of dishes possible. So he'd load it, and then I'd end up rearranging everything before it was ready to go.

Without a doubt, it looked to me like my way was the better way. Tim's way was inefficient, and therefore bad. Yet as my understanding of the Principles grew, I found myself starting to question all the ideas I had about what seemed right and true. I started noticing how self-righteous people can get during an argument, but then when they calmed down, they'd see how skewed, irrational and unreasonable they'd been without realizing it. I started to become more humble and cautious when I'd feel my own self-righteousness set in.

Up until that point, Tim was the one who was turned around and needed to see and do things my way. But as I caught on to how Thought works, it started to look like maybe I was the one that was backwards.

Several things changed for me when I started questioning how I saw our differences. The first change I saw in myself was that the tension and the edge around our differences started to fall away because my mind wasn't wrought with irritation and judgment, and my mind was more open and free.

Here's how that played out when I took a fresh look at the dishwasher issue. When I thought about the fact that he loads the dishwasher in a completely different way, the first thought that hit me was that I think *way* too much about how dishwashers should be loaded. I would love to be as free as my husband and just put things in there and start it and not have to think so much. I would love to not have to think so rigidly about efficiency so I could be more free-spirited and have less on my mind. It was no mystery that overall in his life, Tim was more easygoing and relaxed in all the ways that counted. I wanted to be more like that instead of trying to get him to be more like me. I realized that he seemed to share my values; he just had the perspective to be able to balance efficiency with being easy going, which was what I was missing. Instead of feeling condescending toward him, I started appreciating and admiring the things he had that I didn't. I began realizing those differences are evidence of ways that I could learn from him, and it made me value what Tim brings to our relationship in a whole new way. This brought a level of gratitude and respect into our relationship that was deeper than we'd ever had before.

## Reflection

It sure helps to know that everyone lives in their own Thought-created reality. When people don't understand separate realities, they think that everyone sees the same thing. They frequently ascribe motives to another person's behavior. They take things personally and feel criticized, angry and hurt by the actions of others. A lack of understanding of separate realities can cause relationships to spiral downward, which generates misunderstanding, anger and resentment.

### Mary and Aaron

**Mary:** I was totally devastated when Aaron said he'd been thinking about divorce for a long time. It felt as though I must be in the middle of a car crash. How could that be possible? I scanned my memory, scrambling my brain, to see if I could figure out what he was talking about. Surely, I'm hearing things. He looked at me as if I was the delusional one. Of course, I had to know we were in a dead relationship for years. I tell you, I believe I know what it must feel like to be in the middle of a boxing ring, on the way down.

**Aaron:** I couldn't believe the look on her face when I blurted out the truth we had both been hiding from for so long. Look, I don't want to hurt her; we were good friends. We were never really like husband and wife; we were more like roommates. It was a marriage of convenience from the start.

**Mary:** Our friends can't believe it. They thought we were the perfect couple. In fact, they said they had never known two people to get together so easily and be so good for one another. They said they had never seen Aaron so happy before, either alone or with anyone else for that matter. How could it be that he would feel something so different from me? How could I not know he was so unhappy? Why didn't he ever tell me? Why did he wait so long?

## *Reflection*

It turned out that Aaron was under an enormous amount of stress with a lot of thoughts in his head. He had gotten very insecure and stressed owing to the suicide of a colleague and felt somehow responsible for it. The more he contaminated his innate health with his insecurities, the worse his relationship looked. He had become unhappy but didn't realize it was his thinking making him feel so bad. He thought it was his wife making him feel that way. What seemed like the truth about their relationship was clearly just his thinking. Remember, it looks like truth to the person experiencing it because of the interplay between Thought and Consciousness. This interplay creates the great illusion of life—we're always experiencing our thinking, but we think we're experiencing life.

Aaron eventually allowed himself to consider that his state of mind was obviously colored by his thinking about his buddy's suicide, as well as a host of other thoughts about things from parents, in-laws and everything in between. All of these thoughts influenced his view of his relationship with Mary.

Aaron was in a very low mood and was doing a lot of negative thinking. This is what gave him the experience of being distant from his wife.

All that was necessary is for Aaron to consider that his perspective was not truth but simply Thought, and our thoughts change all the time. They change whether we want them to or not.

It's not at all unusual to hear two completely different stories from two people living together in the same house who have been in a relationship for years—a perfect example of "living in separate realities." Same house, separate realities. It's the way life works given that everyone has different thoughts about things.

## Elsie and Ken

**Ken:** The most important thing for our relationship was understanding separate realities and coming to the realization that having a positive relationship with my wife was more important to me than being right or winning an argument. Otherwise, I probably wouldn't still be sitting here. Over the years I guess I've changed a lot. I was pretty self-centered and didn't think too much beyond my own needs. As I evolved, I saw that I was only half of the relationship, and it was important for both of us to enjoy things. I didn't realize that I was insecure. I honestly thought that I pretty much had it together, and I was right pretty often too. [*laughs*] Obviously I was deluded.

**Elsie:** I forgot that about me too, that I didn't know I was insecure. I just thought I was what I was. I didn't realize it had anything to do with insecurity. I knew I wasn't necessarily happy or content or had peace of mind, but I thought that was just the way I was.

When we first became aware of the Principles, I was still doing my darndest to fix Ken and could not figure out why he wouldn't change. I thought I was doing it with love, and he was reacting to me instead of responding. That started a bit of a divide in our relationship. After a while I started to get a little cheeky with what I thought I knew.

Yeah, it was a rollercoaster ride because even after I started to look at Ken with new eyes and really respect his wisdom and our love deepened, there still were times when I would get into my ego and Ken would get into his ego and we would just come into conflict again. And at one time, Ken and I did separate. We both were caught up in our separate realities at that point, and I personally thought it would be easier being on my own.

And finally, Ken and I talked, and we both agreed that it didn't look like we were getting back together so we may as well formalize this and get divorced.

**Ken:** Somehow, whether Elsie called me after that or whether I called her I don't know, but we started to put feelers out towards each other about getting back together and then we did. We still have our moments, but there's something at the back of your mind telling you, "Relax. This isn't real, and it will go away." And with a clear mind there's enough wisdom to stop you from doing anything irreversible.

It began to dawn on me that having a relationship with Elsie was far more valuable than being right or trying to win an argument. But we weren't at ease with each other at first.

Our relationship has definitely gotten easier since Elsie allows me to live my life the way I want to. Obviously, we're now in tune with each other. It's not like we're going off in opposite directions or anything.

**Elsie:** Yeah, so it's beautiful. I love that feeling between us now. There's just understanding in place, and it's beautiful. The only thing I would just emphasize again is that we've been married fifty years now. It's amazing because I love our relationship more than ever.

And I find Ken still is new to me. There are things that he comes out with that absolutely tickle me and delight me. I love that he sees life from his perspective; that gives me added perspective. And I just love the feeling between us.

# *Reflection*

You can see that after fifty years of marriage, this couple continued to change over time and are now living in a beautiful feeling. Isn't that what we all want—to live with each other in a state of mind that produces deeper feelings of love, respect and harmony.

We have all had the experience of laughing and thinking a movie was hilarious only to hear someone else say it was the worst movie they ever saw—same movie, two totally different experiences. Not only do two people experience the same thing differently, each person will even experience the very same thing differently in different states of mind. We've all had the experience of laughing over something someone said and then later, when your mood has dropped, you recall the conversation but it doesn't seem funny anymore. You start to wonder what the person really meant, as though there was an ulterior motive behind what they said.

The Three Principles explain the illusory quality of Thought. We experience our own creation, and that creation always includes some degree of illusion, colored by our unique perspective. There are infinite personal realities. We can only be in our own heads, no one else's. Even when we describe what is going on very explicitly, we still hear it filtered through our own experience. The more we listen with a quiet mind, the closer we can come to their experience.

## Valda and Keith

**Valda:** There are always times in marriages, at least in our marriage, where we have different ideas about things, how we think about things or what to do about things. Knowing about the Principles gives me an understanding of how we all consistently experience life that is always true. It's like the North Star for me. I am always living in the feeling of my own thinking. That's really powerful for me.

This funny story comes to mind: I remember a time I tried to convince Keith to stack the woodpile in a particular place, but he saw it differently. I really tried to convince him to do it the way I wanted it, but he wasn't interested. No matter what I said or how many times I said it, I couldn't make him change his mind about it. Then at one point I realized, my gosh, I'm experiencing my own upset thinking, not the woodpile. Then the quality of my thinking shifted, and I remembered how much fun it is to be married to Keith, and I was filled with good feelings again. I realized that when I'm having hard feelings and getting upset, it's coming from me—from my own thinking. From that day on, my life experience took a turn.

**Keith:** After Valda had that insight, it changed how she talked to me. I never felt attacked anymore, and I got more relaxed. After that I could really take her in and really listen to her. That one insight meant a world of difference. We were married twenty-five years at that time. Before that there were things that I could not bring up because I would get so upset, and there was clearly going to be an argument.

**Valda:** [laughing] I remember the time I gave Keith a hard time about using the turn signals in his car. I would say, "Why don't you use your turn signals? Use your turn signals." Once again, at some point I realized this is going nowhere and that my upset had something to do with my thinking. Then I softened and instead of being mad, I got curious. I thought how could this lovely, sweet, smart man be such a nitwit when it came to turn signals? Doesn't he realize how dangerous it is and how inconsiderate he's being?

**Keith:** When Valda asked me the next time it came across with a very loving tone, not forced or put on, but genuine. The next thing I knew, I had this huge insight about a time when I was sixteen years old in drivers ed. In my mind, I had questioned why there were so many rules to driving. It looked ridiculous to me, so I decided I could get by and drive perfectly fine without following all their stupid rules. Here it was all these years later, I had no idea that I was operating according to a thought I had when I was sixteen. That insight changed my turn signal behaviors. It wasn't hard. I didn't have to brace myself to change; it became automatic. It didn't take any practice to put it into play. It was just doing what now made perfect sense to me.

**Valda:** So, you never know where you're going to go in your mind, but it's so nice to be able to understand that all of your feelings are always coming from your thinking. You can get a lot of insight about it, and you don't have to feel threatened that someone else can make you feel bad. You can stay settled down even when you have talks that are kind of dicey.

## *Reflection*

When people don't understand separate realities, it doesn't look as though it's Thought that is creating their emotions; it looks as though their thinking is correct, and that's reality. That is the illusion of Thought. Thought and Consciousness are so powerful that our thoughts look real to us in the moment.

Our feelings are always our guide to our state of mind. Knowing this helps us bypass arguments and hurtful interactions. The *feeling* behind the words that come out of our mouths speaks louder than the words.

# Chapter 9

# Freedom From the Past

*The past is a thought carried through time that can distort our life in the present. Memory is Thought in the present of something we think happened in the past. Memories cannot represent the truth, any more than thoughts in the present represent the truth. The only truth is that we have the ability to think, and everything we think appears real and true because of Consciousness. Memory is also colored by the present state of mind. When you are in a more negative state of mind your past could look pretty bad, and when you are feeling better you start to remember good things that happened in your life.*

–Sydney Banks

## Sandy

Growing up I thought that my mother was the cause of my unhappiness. When she introduced me to someone, she would say, "… And this is my mistake," so I started to think of myself as a mistake. That negative thinking distorted how I perceived myself and my life. I was never smart enough, pretty enough, never lovable. I looked at life in terms of what was wrong with me. Whenever she was nice to me, I thought she was just being nice because she felt guilty about not loving me. So no matter what she did, there was no winning with me. Over the years this thinking impacted my ability to have healthy relationships, to feel connected to people. As I started to learn about the Principles, I couldn't let myself think about my past at all because it still looked real to me. One day, I remembered the things my mother used to do for me, and I saw them from a whole different feeling. I started laughing because I realized that I missed out on the really good childhood that I truly had! And what a great mother I had. As I got healthier, my past continued to change because I saw it differently. I realized that I had been insecure, and my mother had been insecure, but it was me who thought I wasn't loveable; it wasn't my mother who thought that. That was the end of my suffering. In fact, thirty years later while visiting my mother, she started laughing over a memory she had about how much she loved me when she was pregnant. It was all in my imagination that she didn't love me. It was just my own thoughts creating an illusion that only appeared to be true to me.

## *Reflection*

This story exemplifies the power that a simple misunderstanding, carried through time from childhood can wreak havoc in one's life and create a negative perception of life. Think about it for a minute: The past doesn't really exist. It is just an illusory memory carried through time that also changes over time. That's profound when you think about it.

This is not to say that bad things haven't happened to people, but what causes them to be traumatic is what we make of the event with our thinking. That thinking can distort how we perceive the present. When you are looking at your present through memories of your painful past, your present can be distorted by those memories without you ever realizing it.

> *Don't go into the past to try to change the present. The sickness is created from innocence—this innocence of life— and believe me, we all suffer from this innocence to one degree or another. Never forget it is forgiveness that washes away all the negative thoughts toward others and allows us to see life in a more positive manner.*
>
> —SYDNEY BANKS

## Yolanda and Jon

Yolanda was a young mother of two and stepparent to three. She had been married to Jon, who was twenty-two years older, and she was very stressed and unhappy. They married when she was twenty, and he was forty-two. She was so in love with him that she agreed to a premarital agreement. Jon had been successful financially, and he wanted to control the finances. At that time, she felt great about everything.

Jon thought that he had been taken advantage of in his first divorce. He had to pay his first wife lots of money, and in the end, he had to care for the children on his own. He was determined not to let another woman do that to him again. When he met Yolanda, he was fearful, and so asked her to sign a prenuptial agreement. Jon's first wife looked like the cause of his suffering, and he held on to his negative memories as a way to protect himself from being hurt if his relationship with Yolanda ended.

Yolanda's father was out of the picture for most of her life, and she grew up yearning for a man's attention. She thought she needed a man who would take care of her. When she fell in love with Jon, she thought that he was giving her the love she always wanted.

As Yolanda matured and became more assertive and self-confident, she started to think about their relationship in a different way. She became stressed and overwhelmed with all the duties she had to take on as the woman of the house. She was frequently tired at night and didn't want to be intimate. She started to think he was taking advantage of her and that she was giving him her best years and would get nothing if he found someone else and left her. Her perception of him changed from her knight in shining armor to perceiving herself as a dependent woman.

They became very reactive, and started fighting and threatening each other. Jon felt Yolanda pull away, and he became afraid she was going to leave him as his first wife had done. He became more controlling and secretive as a result of his perceptions. She saw his behavior as a sign that he had found someone else and was going to leave her if she didn't take care of his needs on demand. They both reacted emotionally, and their relationship spiraled downward.

Yolanda finally asked Jon to come to a couple's session. I talked to them about how Thought worked to create their insecurity, and how the past worked to create problems that weren't really there. As they calmed down and stopped thinking so negatively, they were able to see that they needed to make some changes in how they interacted with one another. Then they were able to reconnect and were back in love in a short time. They both felt so grateful to see how the painful past had distorted their perceptions of each other.

# *Reflection*

Since Yolanda and Jon didn't didn't understand how the Principles worked, they were unaware of what was happening. As they awakened to this realization, they were able to agree on changes in their relationship to make things more equitable. Their problem-solving skills and communication skills improved as their feelings improved.

They were both feeling stressed and insecure because they started thinking about each other in a negative way. Their present situation was distorted by their individual memories of their previous experiences. The more they listened to their negative thoughts, the more real they seemed and their relationship spiraled downward. They each thought their analysis was accurate.

It's easy to think that the past is the source of today's problem. As mentioned earlier, a thought about the past is called a "memory." Since a memory is just a thought, it is only as good as the state of mind we were in when we first experienced it, even we're in when we revisit it in the present.

When people experience hurt feelings, it appears the source of the pain is coming from the words or actions of the other person. It's harder for people to let go of thoughts of the past when they don't understand how Thought works.

It can appear as though the other person intended to inflict pain, even when that's not the case. Even if that is the case, understanding how Thought works would help the person realize that the other person was caught up in their own negative thinking.

> *A calm mind, a silent mind is a mind that is not*
> *contaminated by negative thoughts from the past.*
>
> —SYDNEY BANKS

It makes sense to quiet our minds and bring our awareness to the present moment if we want to feel better. The past is subjective, and memory is not reliable. Memory changes over time and operates according to our state of mind.

We are not saying to never think about the past, but when you understand how Thought works, it's easier to put the past in perspective. Then you can find relief from your suffering and find real peace inside. The truth is we can't help what comes into our minds, but knowing it is only a Thought allows us to reduce our suffering and get back to a clear mind.

Even if your partner brings up something from the past that used to hurt you, if you're truly listening from your heart, it won't have the same affect on you. You'll realize your partner is going there out of their own insecure thinking in that moment, and you won't take it personally. You may even feel compassion. Chances are your partner will then react differently and settle down in the presence of a good feeling. Feeling compassion for your partner will help to diffuse the tension. It's harder to keep an argument going when one other person doesn't engage.

> *If you live in the past, you can never find happiness. You*
> *are trying to live in a reality that no longer exists.*
>
> —SYDNEY BANKS

## Scott

Scott grew up in a family where corporal punishment was the norm. Scott's father would use physical abuse for any infraction of the family rules. When we were first dating, he would tell me stories of his past, and I could feel the pain he felt as he relived each story. After a while when he would start to tell these stories, I would gently change the subject and bring his attention back to the present. One day he asked me, "Why is it that every time I bring up the past, you change the subject?" I told him that his past was now just a thought, brought to life every time he remembered it. Because he didn't see this, I distracted him so that he wouldn't suffer. He thought about that, and about a year later he said to me, "The thing that helped me the most out of everything I learned from you is that my past is just thought."

## *Reflection*

When people have gone through horrendous experiences, such as childhood physical or sexual abuse, rape or other life-threatening events, their current life appears to be negatively affected when they don't have a deeper understanding of how the Principles work. People who work in life-and-death situations, such as veterans, police, military personnel and other first responders, can also be negatively affected when they allow their thoughts to overwhelm them.

Memories can cause significant disruption in a person's ability to be happy and have healthy relationships. Frequently people feel hopeless about finding true happiness or love because they think their ability to experience those feelings comes from what happened to them in the past. Think about it. If you can't see that the past was just a thought, you would think that you are doomed to suffer because of what happened to you. You may think you are broken or damaged, or somehow irrevocably hurt or changed. Absolutely not true because you still have innate health.

## Ed

Ed, a retired police officer, came to see me because the symptoms of his diagnosed PTSD (Post Traumtic Stress Disorder) had become more severe. He was extremely stressed and had a feeling of hopelessness. As soon as he sat down, he went into great detail about his past experiences regarding trauma, treatment, symptoms, nightmares and awkward social interactions. For about twenty minutes he told me everything he knew to be true, including the fact that his PTSD was so severe that he was hopeless. He put a lot of effort into convincing me of the severity of his condition. His voice had an anxious edge, and his words were forceful and fast paced.

Knowing what I did about the Principles, I sat with a relaxed feeling, listening without thinking about the content of what he was saying. At one point a thought popped in my head and I said, "Can I ask you a question?" He said "Yes." I asked, "How often throughout the day do you think about your PTSD?" Ed got this strange puzzled look on his face and appeared incredulous. I've seen this look many times before in my thirty years of law enforcement experience, and it clearly portrayed, "Are you an idiot or something?"

After taking a moment to get himself under control so as to appear polite, he said, "What do you mean?" I replied, "How often throughout the day do you go into the details of what you think you know about yourself and your PTSD?" At this he became animated and angrily raised his voice and said, "All the time! Do you think I want to take my wife hostage again and this time kill her or be killed by my police partners?" For about twenty minutes or so, he continued to talk in great detail about why he needed to think about his PTSD to keep his wife and himself safe.

Suddenly, he stopped talking and sat in silence for a moment. His demeanor seemed to change, and he had a look of being puzzled. In a soft, slow voice he said, "Are you saying that if I thought less about my PTSD, I would feel better?" I said, "I don't know. Is that what I'm saying?" Silence reigned for a short time.

As I watched him, it looked like a load began to be lifted from his shoulders. He became more relaxed, and then he said in a calm, slow-paced voice, "That's what I heard you say. I'm going to try it."

A week later, Ed walked into my office. He looked like a different person. He was smiling and upbeat. He sat down and said, "You know how last week you said to stop being so negative?" (I had not said this.) "I stopped listening to the negative talk radio channels, watching the negative news and telling negative stories to my friends. I feel wonderful!" For the next fifty minutes he told me all the wonderful thoughts that were coming to mind for him and how many possibilities were coming to mind that he hadn't seen before. He said that he felt closer to his wife than he had in years and that she was "ecstatic" with how he felt and how he was acting.

Ed's quieter state of mind allowed him to see what he was doing to himself as the thinker. I saw him a few more times, and his life continued to change in a positive way. We spoke again months later, and he said that it wasn't as if he didn't get upset and lose his balance on a regular basis, but after seeing a glimpse of the Principles and seeing how they worked to create his experience, it became difficult to sustain the idea that it was something outside of his thinking that was making him angry or anxious. He equated this with a "daymare" and said he now knew that the key was to wake up, not get into the details of the horrors he was creating in his head. He still had bad dreams but said that after a short time they looked like dreams without any major significance.

## Reflection

You can see how the past can affect a person if they don't see that the past is just Thought. People sometimes end up getting divorced because their past creates such an illusion that they accuse their partner of things that happened to them previously in their life.

Memory can work to protect us and keep us safe. That is why we remember not to touch a hot stove. When we experience events that are life threatening, our memories of these situations can cause a distortion in a current situation. The more we are thinking from this insecure state of mind, the more we innocently access those memories and the more real they appear in the present. Frequently the anxiety a person carries from these memories after the event is over is worse than when it actually happened. You can see how understanding that feeling can have positive affect on you and your relationships. It can free you from your painful or traumatic past.

> *Seek a clear understanding of the past; realize that the*
> *negative feelings and emotions from past traumatic*
> *experiences are no longer true. They are merely memories,*
> *a collection of old stale thoughts.*
>
> –SYDNEY BANKS

## Katie

Katie came to see me because she continued to get into relationships with men who treated her in controlling and demeaning ways. At this time, she had been in two relationships with men who both felt a sense of ownership over her. They would make her dress in certain ways, only agree to see her at specific times or days and demanded that she cater to their bizarre requests. She came in because she knew something must be off within her because she continued to get into relationships that were so strange. As we talked, she told me that her father was mentally ill and had sexually abused her from age nine to thirteen. Katie said, "But this didn't affect me because I knew this wasn't him doing it. I knew his mental illness and alcoholism made it seem okay to do what he did. I knew it wasn't my fault. I knew I wasn't bad, and I knew he wouldn't be doing this if he was in his right mind. So I don't think that it affected me." After listening, I told her that she may not have been affected in the most common ways, but she certainly did have a lot of tolerance for bad behavior in insecure men.

# Reflection

This is a good story of how someone's thinking creates a reaction to trauma. Katie's wisdom at the time of the traumatic event helped her see that her father's behavior was not personal to her. She knew that she wasn't responsible for what her father did, but other thinking allowed her to tolerate abusive behavior even though she didn't take it personally. Her wisdom led her to seek counseling because she *KNEW* that something wasn't right about her relationships with men. As Katie understood how the Principles were creating her view of relationships with men, she began to *SEE* how her thinking from the past was affecting her in the present.

# Section 3

# Unlock the Mystery

*Love and forgiveness go hand in hand. Without them, life
is encumbered by ill feelings and unhappiness.*

—SYDNEY BANKS

**Keith:** Knowing about the Principles has enabled us to have conversations
and work through things. Knowing where our feelings are coming from has
made all the difference. We've been able to tackle thorny issues and all sorts
of difficulties and really get somewhere with it just by being on each other's
side. We're able to move through uncharted territory and talk about anything without getting hurt or getting stuck in our old ways.

# Chapter 10

# Innocence: Seeing Through the Eyes of Love

*Regardless of how the mind of humanity is lost or what behavioral pattern this mental lostness may take, it all derives from the wrongful usage of the Three Principles.*

–SYDNEY BANKS

## Bob

Growing up, I thought my father did not care about me because he refused to help me with my homework. There was always some excuse. It felt as though he just could not be bothered with me. Pops would say, "I don't have my glasses; I can't help you now," or "I don't have the time now; I'm busy."

Throughout elementary school I had little respect for my father, so I questioned him a lot and behaved like an oppositional, difficult child, causing severe clashes between my father and me. All of this was set in motion by my assumption that my father must not love or care about me because he refused to help me with my homework. Then, at some point in my twenties, I learned that my father was actually unable to read and write! I could hardly believe it. How could that be possible since I had seen him read the newspaper?

Pops admitted with great embarrassment that he was not actually reading the paper; he was trying to teach himself to read. I said, "But what about when you read the Bible? I know that you can read the Bible." My father was able to read the Bible and loved to do so.

I suddenly felt so much compassion and love for my father; I said: "Pops, if you can read the Bible, then you can read the newspaper. They are the same words just in a different order." Luckily, Pops was open-minded enough to hear the common sense in my statement, and we both had a big insight that he just had a mental block about the newspaper. He thought that reading a newspaper was beyond a person without an education, yet he had always thought the Bible was written for everyone, not just the educated elite.

## *Reflection*

Can you see that one little misunderstanding can generate years of ill will and bad feelings all quite innocently? As soon as the misunderstanding was corrected, both parties had huge insights, creating a whole new relationship.

One important piece of information blew this lifelong illusion right out of Bob's head, and his father was able to read the newspaper with much greater ease and enjoyment. Bob's view of his father completely changed in that moment. He realized that his father had used all those excuses so he didn't have to admit that he couldn't read. It wasn't because he didn't care about Bob, quite the contrary. Bob was able to apologize for his orneriness as a youth, and his Pops understood. Their whole relationship changed with one revelation. This is the secret that unlocks the mystery. It is our own thinking that holds us back. We innocently hold on to thinking that what we believe is true, therefore contaminating our loving feeling even though those thoughts are not valid.

By innocence we're not talking about being guilty or innocent. This innocence is a person's inability to see life any differently than how they currently see it. People often do things that appear to be vindictive, hurtful or manipulative. They are really only trying to gain relief for themselves. Whatever they think, do or say is a product of the insecure state of mind they are currently experiencing. They are not aware of their own behavior much of the time.

People generally don't make the connection between what's happening in their lives and what's happening in their heads. They don't know that what they're feeling and seeing is coming from within them. As a result, people tend to keep thinking silly, disturbing, troubled thoughts that seem real and true. The more people think these thoughts, the more real they seem and the more true they appear. Without understanding how reality works, people can easily be tricked by the illusion of Thought. They may become violent or do hurtful things without even realizing what they are doing because they are too caught up in their own perspective of what's happening.

All of us can awaken to see that innate health is always there beneath the negative thoughts. We were born with the capacity to live in a state of mind where loving is effortless and natural, where we can decide what to pay attention to and what not to pay heed to. That is true free will.

We're not saying that staying in a dangerous or toxic situation is a good idea. But if you get into a healthy state of mind, you will see what you need to do to stay healthy. This could mean many things. No one can know what you should do but you. Your innate wisdom will always direct you to health and safety.

When we're in a beautiful state of mind where love and compassion exist, it feels wonderful. It is also the place where we get good, healthy ideas that move life in a positive direction. There are no rules. Everyone is is different. You will know what to do if you listen to and trust your common sense.

## Sherilyn and Jacob

Sherilyn said that her husband, Jacob, disappoints her often because she expects him to think about getting her a card and a gift for special occasions; that's how she was raised.

Jacob said, "I've gotten much better about that because I know it's important to her, but I was raised to work hard and provide a good income for my family. It doesn't always occur to me to remember special occasions because I'm so focused on my work."

Sherilyn said, "We've been together fifteen years; don't you think he'd know what I want by now?"

# *Reflection*

Can you see that Sherilyn had expectations (thoughts) about what her partner should do for her so she could feel loved, special, important and so on? However, Jacob did not have those same thoughts. She thought he should know better because they'd been together for fifteen years. But the truth of the matter is time doesn't matter. What is important is our personal thinking. In this case, Jacob thought the fact that he worked to provide for her should be enough to make her happy.

Not recognizing how Thought works to create their individual ways of seeing life led to their upset. They judged each other based upon their own expectations, which caused their distress and resulted in dissonance within their relationship.

In addition, when Jacob didn't give her presents or cards, Sherilyn thought that meant he didn't love her very much. Had she seen her husband's innocence, the outcome would have been different. We all have beliefs and rituals that we pick up from others or from the family in which we were raised. We then assume that's how everyone does things. Understanding that this is the nature of thought changes everything. Had she realized that he was paying attention to earning a good living for them, she would have realized that was his way of giving to her. So he really did care about her; he was just not in the habit of paying attention to special occasions. What a difference that revelation would have made for this couple. Knowing that people are often blind to things that are completely obvious to others, propels a person to ask rather than jump to conclusions from their personal vantage point.

# Chapter 11

# Forgiveness

*I remember someone telling me he could never forgive
his Dad because his Dad was alcoholic, and when he got
drunk he would beat him. He said he could never possibly
forgive his Dad—to me that was sad. Suddenly, he realized
what his Dad must be going through, not just him, but
his Dad—to be going through this awful state. It was like
a light switched on in his head, and he suddenly burst out
crying.*

*It was the first time in his life that he felt love for his Dad
and now he and his Dad are the best of friends. To me,
that's a real success story because this person didn't just
find the innocence toward his Dad, since he was the finder
he projected this innocence to everybody else in life—just
because he saw the innocence of his Dad.*

–SYDNEY BANKS

## Micaela

I divorced my first husband, Steven, because of several affairs, alcohol dependence, emotional abuse and his severe depression. I decided to remain in a good feeling with my ex so that our son would not be more impacted by the divorce than was necessary. Steven got sober twenty years ago but continued to struggle with failed relationships and depression. During the twenty-five years we had been divorced, I had taken him in as a boarder five times. He would become suicidal and destitute, and I would always welcome him in. His health would return, his life would get better and he would move out again. I genuinely like him and had forgiven him, understanding that he was living in an illusion that made it look like the things he did were good ideas. I raised our son to know that his dad was doing the best he could see how to do and that if he could be a more present father, he would be. The last time Steven stayed with me I shared what I knew about the Principles, and he started to listen. Now, he is on his way to a more sustained level of well-being and is learning how the Principles work in him. He is now employed, in a long-term relationship and generally managing his life in a way that is positive and productive. I continue to get emails from him telling me how he's changing and getting healthier. This is the gift I gave my son so that he would have a father who is healthy and able to be available to him. It's also a gift I gave myself so I don't have to carry around the insecurity and hurt that I had in the past.

## *Reflection*

You're probably thinking that Micaela must be a saint and that she has all the reason in the world to feel angry and resentful toward her ex-husband. She was able to realize that carrying around resentful and judgmental thinking would only continue to hurt herself and her son. Plus, Micaela knew that Steven was acting out of an unhealthy state of mind, and if he regained his bearings he wouldn't make such poor choices.

Forgiveness really only helps the person doing the forgiving. It wouldn't help the person they are forgiving unless that person also forgave him- or herself. In other words, forgiveness by itself doesn't help the person being forgiven. They have to have their own insight.

Forgiveness gives us hope. When you forgive, it lets you off the hook, allows you freedom to start anew and makes you feel better. When you continue to think about what happened that seems unforgivable, you're just holding yourself a prisoner of the past. Recognizing the innocence in others, no matter what their behavior, will come to you as your level of consciousness rises. Then you may totally forget about it.

Have you ever felt compassion for someone while they were yelling at you? Perhaps a boss, a parent, your spouse? All it took was one compassionate thought, such as "the poor dear, must have had a really bad day today." In that moment, you've seen the person's innocence—they are unaware of the fact that their anger is coming from their thinking, not from you! In relationships there are always other variables at play that we cannot know. You may discover later that her husband asked for a divorce the night before or his son was in a terrible accident. Compassionate thoughts come to us when we don't personalize their words or behaviors. This doesn't mean you are forgiving what they did. You see it from a different vantage point.

# Chapter 12

# The Hidden Troublemaker in Every Relationship

*Ego is only what you think you are and what you think of life, nothing more, nothing less.*

–Sydney Banks

## Tom

I suppose like many people, my thinking about myself pretty much picked what I did in my life. I had learned to misuse this wonderful gift of Thought to create a story around who I thought I was. I didn't realize that how I had been thinking wasn't healthy, and so the story I had created wasn't healthy either.

When it came to intimate relationships, my insecure thinking worked like radar. I would go into a room, and within a few minutes, I would see potential date material. [*laughs*] It typically had nothing to do with who these people were. It had more to do with how they looked. My sense of self-importance had a lot to do with how I looked. I attached my worth and the woman's worth to my thinking about looks.

So in my single years, I would walk into a room looking for the physically attractive women. I remember a time when I was at an outdoor dance in Michigan. I saw this really pretty girl, and I went up to her and started talking to her and her friend. Her friend didn't appear as pretty, but I remember having much more of a connection with her. For a minute I thought, "It's more fun talking to the friend," and I wondered if I should pursue her. But then I squashed that idea. So I spent the rest of the night with the other lady. It wasn't that much fun, but I really felt good about myself. Of course, at that time I thought this high feeling was caused by the pretty woman. What I didn't realize was that it was my own thinking, telling me how good I was because this beautiful lady was paying attention to me.

So I would get involved with these pretty women, and then two things would happen. I'd realize that there really wasn't a soul-mate connection, and I kept searching looking for more, better or different. I was constantly trying to prove myself, so I would be with these pretty women and then I'd see another pretty woman and then another pretty woman. This thinking bashed me around. I was miserable, and I didn't realize that my misery was caused by my insecure thinking. I thought I must really love these people or why would I feel so horrible.

On two occasions, I asked these ladies to marry me. I was pretty good at persuading them, not from health but from insecurity. They said yes, and we got married. I married two women who were very nice, but I didn't marry them out of my health; I married them out of my egotistical thinking. So, there I was, and what do you do then? Well I was fairly fortunate that I ended up being an idiot, and they had enough evidence to divorce me. I guess the fortunate part was it happened before we had any children. And, before I had any money [*laughs*], so I got lucky.

Then I had the thought—you know, something's wrong here. I'm a psychologist, and I'm doing all this crap. I started therapy, and I guess I got a little bit better. I didn't know why I felt better though, so I still kept looking for this type of woman. And I probably could have gotten married two or three more times, except the women wouldn't take me back after I wandered, which was fortunate.

Then finally I experienced the Principles. I began to catch on about life. I realized that I was the leading character in a story of myself that I made up. All of a sudden, I saw that I could put some distance between me and my thinking.

Then came a little bit of wisdom, and I began to realize that I am not what I think of myself. I understood what was going on; it was almost like breaking an addiction. My life began to change. I started spending time with different people; I wasn't caught up in having to prove myself anymore. I decided that I wasn't going to be in a relationship unless there was a good feeling about it. Actually, I realized that I could be happy whether I was in a relationship or not. And that was real freedom for me. You know, I was still looking because I think when people are happy they want to share it with somebody. But for the first time I didn't have to.

One day I responded to an ad from an Asian lady named Susan. We sat down, and I found her attractive; there were things about her that resonated with me. She didn't have much to say though. Since I didn't really need to be in a relationship, at one point I said, "You've been really quiet; maybe you are just not that attracted to me, and that's okay." But, she responded and said, "Well maybe I'm just nervous." I liked that. It was so honest and open that I felt more attracted after that.

I took Susan to a party where my friends met her. I thought it was a really good evening, but the next day I listened to a message on my answering machine from Erin, one of my female friends who was at the party. She said, "Hi Tom. It was nice to see you at the party, but where did you find her? Was she cleaning your hotel room? Did you see her teeth?" The first feeling I had was anger, but I let that go.

The next time that I saw Susan, I looked at her teeth. She kind of had big teeth, and they were a little buck. I hadn't noticed before, but after my friend said this, all of a sudden, I started noticing and I got a tremendous amount of anxiety. Then I started noticing other things about her that weren't the way I would have liked them to be. But the good thing was that I saw Thought for what it was.… It was really powerful. Thought was what was creating my experience because before I hadn't even noticed Susan's teeth, and so it didn't have a negative effect on me. In the past I probably would've started looking around again, but I didn't because I knew it was my thinking. And so I didn't honor it like I used to.

I have to tell you that sometimes I got worked up by it. There were moments when I thought, *I don't know if I can take this.*

We're married now, and I've learned to love Susan's teeth. It just doesn't bother me anymore. Those thoughts don't ever come up. The beauty of our relationship is really the result of understanding these Principles. I can't believe we've been together now eleven years, and I see her every day as fresh and new as the day before. I didn't think that was possible. And it certainly wouldn't have been had I still been living in the thinking I opened this story up with.

# *Reflection*

You can see how insecure thinking causes trouble. The way we think about ourselves sometimes creates the perception that we're better than other people or sometimes worse than other people. Two sides of the same coin: I'm not lovable, or I'm better than everyone else. Either way you are placing yourself at the center of the universe with your own thinking.

The problem for many of us is that we have thoughts about ourselves that are based on insecurity and negativity. When these thoughts are engaged, we frequently end up doing or saying things that can create a bad feeling in us and create big problems in our lives. You can't get away from thinking about yourself and your life, but you can see it for what it is—nothing!

In the moment that we recognize our difficult experience is coming to us from our own thinking, we are free. We are free to look for a better feeling about ourselves and our lives.

People who understand how the Principles work tend to cut others more slack because they know, in that moment, the person is simply caught up in their thinking about themselves and their life. They are acting according to how they are thinking. In fact, an upset person really wants understanding. Yet when they get caught up in self-righteous thinking, the last thing their partner wants to do is care for them. Typically, their partner will become defensive or walk away.

It's always our thinking that creates our suffering, whether in the short term or the long term. For example, someone might say something to you, and you laugh about it at the time, but then later you think, "Wait a minute I wonder what they really meant by that?" Or you might start thinking, "Of all the nerve; how dare they?" When we don't realize the feeling is coming from our *own* thinking, we take it personally and ascribe motive to others. During these times, we tend to get the most tricked by our thinking because it looks like something is being done to us or was said intentionally to hurt us.

The more personal the comment seems to be, the more we're being tricked by our insecure personal thinking. If someone said, "You have pink polka dots on your face," you wouldn't take it personally because you know you don't look that way. But if you think you're a little overweight and someone mentions that you've put on some weight, you would probably take that personally and feel resentful because you already think it's true.

The knowledge that we are whole and innately healthy, no matter what someone else says or does, allows us the freedom not to suffer over the negative words and actions of others. Our common sense will guide us when dealing with people who may be caught up in their own negative, insecure thinking.

> *Never hold negative thoughts against each other.*
> *Never hold negative thoughts against each other from the past.*
>
> —SYDNEY BANKS

# Chapter 13

# The Illusion of Thought

*To anybody looking for happiness, don't blame your wife, don't blame your husband, don't blame your child, don't blame your situation; look at your thought, look at how you think. Once your thinking process is upgraded, that's where your higher level of Consciousness is. If you can upgrade your thinking process, you'll start to find your happiness and release yourself from the bonds of yesterday.*

—Sydney Banks

## Kara

I was about to leave the house one evening to run to the store. I wasn't sure if I had enough time before dinner, so I asked my husband, Drew, who was cooking, how long before dinner would be ready. I predicted in my mind that he'd respond, "in a few" or "shouldn't be too long" or some other vague, non-committal reply, the way he always does. I felt myself gear up for another vague response. Sure enough, Drew answered, "pretty soon." And predictably, I got really impatient and irritated.

However, on this one occasion, instead of my impatience running away with me, it suddenly occurred to me, "Why is it his job to be clear? Why wouldn't it be my job to be more patient?" This thought had never occurred to me before. Up until that point, every time he gave me a vague answer, I'd get irritated. And from that state, it looked to me like the fault was 100 percent on him.

I had been working under the assumption that being vague is not helpful, that it wastes time because it forces me to ask a bunch of follow-up questions to extract the information I need. So I felt justified in being irritated. But in that moment, I realized that my impatience was actually a waste of time too, maybe a bigger one.

Once my head cleared and my upset went away, the situation solved itself. I asked the obvious question, which was, "What do you mean by pretty soon?" He took a second, and replied, "About 15 minutes," and I had all the information I needed. No argument, no snide remarks, no defensiveness. The fact that the conversation went so smoothly made it clear that the problem had ultimately come from me and my thinking. It turned out I was the one wasting time being upset and creating tension. And yet all this time I'd been blaming him.

What's interesting to me is that, I find myself surprisingly flexible and easygoing about the way other people are in my life. I factor in their predictable habits. I find ways of working around those habits, and I don't take them personally. When things don't go my way at work, in my parenting or with my friends, it's really not a big deal.

In retrospect, I have a new appreciation for how well Drew has handled my predictable habit of getting impatient and irritated. In this instance, he was living much more gracefully in the understanding of the Principles than I was because he didn't take my irritation personally. In his mind, it was clearly my problem, and he didn't really concern himself with it the way I didn't concern myself with my friend's lateness. As I saw that about him, it freed me.

This insight shifted my thinking about Drew as "the issue." I shifted away from seeing it as a relationship issue and saw it as a by-product of my experience of the relationship. This allowed my relationships to be ultimately easier, to be closer and to be more connected.

## Reflection

As people understand that they are creating their emotional experience by what they think of their relationship, they realize no one and nothing is to blame. They realize they are being tricked by their own thinking even though it feels as though their emotions are caused by the other person rather than from their perception (personal thinking) of the person or situation. Once people begin to see that it's their thinking that distorts life's events, they can stop blaming the other person. It's the great illusion of Thought.

As people begin to see how Thought works, they automatically take responsibility for their own actions because they see it is their thinking that leads them there, not the other person. However, we don't have to be led by our thinking. When we know that feelings are there to guide us, we can use our feelings of anger, for example, as a signal to calm down rather than lash out.

Using feelings as a *guide* to your current state of mind is much different from trying to control your feelings. People talk about anger management, thinking they have to control anger that is justifiable. If your angry feelings appear justifiable, you'll know that you're being tricked by your own thinking. In other words, you're always reacting to your thinking never the outside world, which is true for everyone whether they know it or not.

> *Any negativity in your relationship is created by you.*
> —Sydney Banks

## Juan and Felicia

Juan and Felicia had been together since they were eighteen years old. They had two children and a comfortable life. Juan had become very insecure in his relationship because he found out that when they were first dating, Felicia dated another boy. He had been suspicious of this at the time, but she lied about it because it didn't mean anything to her, and she had only recently told him the truth.

He became anxious, angry and depressed. Juan began questioning what Felicia was doing all day, checking her phone records, monitoring her voice and text messages and calling to check up on her. He questioned her love for him and her commitment to their relationship. Felicia thought he was crazy because she had been loyal and faithful from the day they were married. She lost her patience with him and started to get angry and distant, which caused him to feel more insecure. Juan then saw her behavior as validation of his beliefs about her. Things spiraled downward, and they started fighting almost every day.

Felicia thought she couldn't take it anymore and forced Juan to talk to a therapist. In the first session, he began to explain why he was acting as he was. He was so convincing that he had me thinking she might be having an affair! Then I realized that this incident happened twelve years ago, prior to their marriage! I helped him to see how insecure thoughts created his jealousy and how he saw what he was thinking, not what was real. He could see that the more he thought about his fears about Felicia, the more real it appeared and the more controlling and suspicious he became in response to the illusion. He was like a hunter (which happened to be his hobby) searching for prey, trying to catch his wife.

When Juan realized what he was doing, he calmed down and started to laugh at himself. He had not realized that his thoughts could create such a distortion. As his mind quieted down, he was able to relax and focus on the positive moments between them and appreciate how wonderful his life was now. He even said that meeting Felicia had saved his life because she helped him to be responsible and more secure.

## Reflection

This is an example of how Thought creates an illusion and makes what happened in the past still appear to be real. Juan was so convinced that an affair was happening in the present that he also almost convinced his therapist. You can see that when we tell other people what we think, we can be so convincing that they believe it too, which perpetuates the seeming reality of the illusion. It becomes a self-fulfilling truth. The lie gets perpetuated innocently.

I'm reminded of a counseling session with another couple. He said, "I realized that my worry/thinking made everything look suspect!" That kind of thinking makes it appear as though things external to my own thoughts have to be dealt with, changed or somehow controlled when, in fact, I'm just trying to change something that was created by my own thinking.

> *My mother used to tell me if I was worrying about*
> *something bad that might happen, "That's just a play you*
> *wrote, being performed over and over all in your head."*
>
> –Anonymous

## Sam and Jean

Sam and Jean were on the verge of divorcing after thirty years of marriage. Sam had convinced himself that he had no choice but to leave the marriage, so much so that he would not even agree to come to a joint session with Jean. They did, however, agree to come in individually.

Sam had recently had a life-threatening medical problem around the time of his 60th birthday. He began thinking about the remainder of his life, realizing that it was, in fact, time limited. Sam concluded that he was no longer willing "to take all the abuse" (as he put it) from his wife. According to Sam, he had endured Jean's outbursts, irrational anger and a need to always get her way throughout their marriage. He said he had kept quiet, waiting for it to pass, and he learned to just give in to her so that she would stop yelling. He added that even though the majority of the things he gave into her about were not earth shattering, he thought he had compromised his desires for thirty years.

Jean admitted that she did get angry but only when she'd had enough of "his need to control everything." From her point of view, Sam ran the show. She said that friends agreed with her. However, Jean's view had been that it really didn't matter that much. She thought he was a great father and a hard worker, so what's the big deal if she went along with what he wanted as far as how much money he thought they could afford for things, where they went on vacation, how they spent weekends and so on.

She saw him as passive, socially insecure and pensive, but she looked past all of these character traits because she loved him and chose to focus on his strengths. She had figured that since she was an outgoing person, she took the lead in their minimal social life and didn't mind staying home most evenings to match Sam's social inhibitions.

Sam eventually realized that he dealt with his insecurities by taking control wherever possible. Sam's controlling behavior had been hidden from him in his "blind spot" since he felt so out of control. In his view, Jean would throw a temper tantrum whenever she didn't get her way.

He was unaware of all the times she was "giving in" to his desires because she never spoke about them. They weren't important enough to her to speak with him about them.

From Jean's perspective, she would have to become "emphatic" in order to get her way on things that really were important to her. Sam's perspective was that she had temper tantrums to get her way and said, "Her explosions were completely out of line," and he couldn't stand for it any longer.

## Reflection

It became crystal clear that Jean's "emphatic" was Sam's "out of control, irrational anger." This is an example of how each person's thinking was creating their own reality and how they each had a different reality. Sam began to HEAR Jean's upset as opposed to hearing his own thoughts about her.

When people get curious about their partner's view of things, they will avoid jumping to conclusions on their own. Imagine how things would be different in anyone's relationship if they saw that their partner's behavior was *always* about what's going on in their individual minds rather than thinking their partner was impacting them by creating their bad feelings.

## *Misunderstanding Leads to Common Pitfalls in Relationships*

Dr. George Pransky, PhD., one of the founding psychologists of Principle-based counseling and the author of *The Relationship Handbook,* said he guessed that about 90 percent of people who have come to him for help over the years came for one of three reasons:

- an inability to handle the emotionally reactivity of their partner,
- conflict over differences that build on each other, and
- things in the relationship that are different than what they expected.

Let's have a closer look at these three reasons for relationship problems.

## Emotional Reactivity

Emotional reactivity means reacting to the outside world as if our emotional experience is coming from the event or the person. In a relationship, one person or the other might react to things that their partner doesn't understand. They frequently develop blind spots about their experience. It's important to understand that most people can get emotionally reactive from time to time, but everyone is capable of catching their reaction when they realize they're responding negatively. We are all gifted with resilience. We can change our minds. If you know how Thought works, you'll recognize that your reactivity is coming from your state of mind, not the other person. If you're feeling tired, stressed or overwhelmed, you are more likely to have an emotional reaction. Knowing this could help you pay attention when you start to react, and you'll know to calm yourself down. Knowing how to compose yourself allows for an opportunity to be more graceful in life. It just takes a simple adjustment. Some days you might have to make lots of adjustments, like hitting a reset button, over and over and over again.

A lot of people think they have a bad temper, as though a bad temper is a thing to be managed. They might think their temper is just a part of their personality or in their genetic makeup. None of that is true. A bad temper is simply the result of people taking insecure and negative thinking seriously in the moment. Sometimes people get angry if they feel threatened or perceive themselves as being treated unfairly by someone else. Whatever you think is the cause of your anger or frustration, or if you think you are being victimized in some way, it's always your own thinking that you're reacting to even when it appears as though someone or something else in your life is doing it to you.

As far as the emotional reactivity of others, remember that the same thing is taking place for them. When people feel anger, they are always upset by their own thinking. It's not your job to live your life trying to make others happy because that is simply not possible. It's not about you! It doesn't matter who's having the emotional reaction, the answer is always the same: calm down and wait for wisdom to show you what to do.

## Fred and Emma

Fred and Emma were both divorcees and had been living together for several years with little conflict. Fred was suddenly in the position to get his children back full time. They both agreed to bring the children to their house and to start the process of building a new family unit. As things usually go, the changes were met with stress, and everyone struggled to maintain their emotional balance.

Fred started to get frustrated with the teenage boys and would have episodes where he was emotionally reactive to their lack of respect for Emma and the house rules. He would start to talk to them about what needed to change, and as he talked, he would listen to himself and get even more angry as he spoke. Soon this laid-back fellow started using four-letter words and becoming verbally abusive. Emma tried to step in and calm him down, but once he was in blast-off mode he couldn't hear much. They came in for counseling because Emma did not want to continue in the relationship if their problems couldn't be resolved.

## *Reflection*

Emma was interested in helping everyone be happy. Fred knew that he got angry but didn't realize how much it frightened others. He didn't realize that he was listening to his own thoughts about the situation. As he thought about the situation, his thinking got progressively worse, and things looked more and more personal. He would spiral into an emotionally reactive state of mind, and it seemed to him that he was being mistreated and disrespected.

Emma realized that she was scaring herself with her thoughts about angry men. She started judging Fred and feeling fearful that she would become the focus of his anger. As she realized that her fear was coming from her thoughts and not from Fred, she was able to intervene and talk to Fred in a way that allowed him to see that he also could be different. As they both quieted down, they were able to see how their thoughts had tricked them into thinking that the outside reality was creating their upset.

They both wanted to live in a beautiful feeling, and as they awakened to the Principles, they were able to use their upset as a signal to calm down and wait to address the situation from a more loving place.

> If the only thing people learned was not to be afraid of their experience that alone would change the world.
>
> —SYDNEY BANKS

## Conflict over Differences

Remember that differences are only thoughts that people have created based on their life experiences. These thoughts create completely different perceptions and frequently change with time.

If you want to find magic in your relationship, try not to concern yourself with your differences. Differences only become roadblocks when we are attached to our personal perceptions. If we realize that our likes and dislikes are just thoughts and that we each think differently, then it's no big deal that we see things differently. Look for anything you can find that interests you about how your partner could perceive something so radically differently from you, even if you've been married fifty years to the same person.

Listening to different opinions can open you up to things you've not been aware of previously. At times it may seem that those opinions are so different you'd swear the person is from a different planet, and sometimes that extraterrestrial is your partner. If you get curious about a person's thinking and their line of reasoning, then you will begin to see things as they do, and as a result, you will realize there are no negative motives behind their thoughts or actions.

Now, you may wish to decide what you are willing to live with and what you are not. It's not that difficult to live with someone who prefers eating steak over fish, but what about someone who believes that "partying" (getting drunk) every night is their lifestyle and expects you to condone it? Or what if your life is in danger? We are all gifted with free will, and we can simply decide what we are willing to accept and what we are not. Anyone can love another person dearly and still not be able to live with them.

## Molly

I'd been divorced for twenty some odd years when I met Noah, who seemed to be my polar opposite. However, I felt "chemistry" that I had not felt during most of those years, even though I had met many men and been on countless dates. It seemed so preposterous to me that this man would pop into my head at the most inopportune times—I had work to do and men to date, by golly. But then I remembered what the Principles tell me: Since I create my experience from within, it's all up for grabs…so then I thought, "Why not grab for some gusto?" The Principles also taught me that he had his experience, and I had mine; we are each on our own journey here. At that point our differences became nothing more than an interesting story to witness. Me, the artsy hippy chick from San Francisco; Noah, a corporate finance guy. He, type A with a capitol A; me, type B most of the time. Me, out of a relationship for a long time after a short-term marriage; he, out for a brief time after a long-term marriage. Me, ready to shower a man with all the love and affection stored up for years; he, with his heart walled off I presumed out of protection over whatever thinking he had going on—fear of giving in to someone, fear of trusting any woman other than a family member, no bandwidth remaining beyond what he willingly gave to his children. Whatever Noah's thinking was causing his ability or lack thereof to give to a woman who was not blood related, I knew it was coming from him. Whether in his blind spot or not, it was still his production, having nothing to do with me.

Our list of differences went on and on, even in the way we thought about life. What I realized is that differences have absolutely no bearing on the feeling I can have if I don't pay attention to differences! Learning that I can only feel my own thinking helped me not take any of it personally. Why on earth would I want to create a bad feeling, which I surely would if I focused on our differences? If the feeling is good, nothing else really matters. In the past, differences would have been a deal breaker for me. It is so freeing to be able to spend time with someone with absolutely no expectations for him to change. He is on his journey here, and I am on mine. It's incredibly freeing to just enjoy what there is to enjoy and leave the rest behind, to focus on enjoyment and take the focus off differences and perceived needs. A big lesson learned. It is never up to the other person to give us what we desire, even if our desires have seemingly reached gargantuan proportions. Desires are self-imposed via our personal thinking, too! And my experience with Noah, who remained quite distant, was the catalyst for all of these insights. We are always in a relationship with our own thinking, and I could fall in love with my own mind and the extraordinary insights that came to me.

I realized I could enjoy myself without having any skin in the game, so to speak. It's all up to me and what I make of life's events. Understanding how the Principles work within everyone has made an enormous difference in my life, and it's been the greatest blessing of my life. I wish it for everyone.

## *Reflection*

Even though this is a story from a single person, it is equally applicable for any relationship. Any two people will find enormous differences in the way they think about things. As we talked about it in the section on Separate Realities, what you see is coming from you, from your thoughts, which is why your opinions look so good to you.

One caveat: If you are considering separation or divorce over differences, make sure that you are not caught up in your own personal insecurity when making a decision. It's easy to think that splitting up is the only way you can feel better. That's another illusion of your own making. Ask your partner what he or she thinks first, and think about the impact it might have on your children. People who split up with love and understanding and take their children's feelings into account will create the best outcome for their children. It's better for children to have divorced parents that respect each other's differences but still decide the best solution is to go their separate ways. Children will pick up animosity even if you think you're hiding it. There is no need to hide animosity when there is an understanding that everyone is truly doing the best they see to do given how they perceive things.

## Expectations

Beware of expectations you may hold in your thinking. They are just thoughts we make up about how we think our relationship will play itself out. When real life happens and it differs from our imaginary thoughts, we are disappointed because we don't realize that what we made up came from our imagination. Sometimes we think relationships should be the way they are in the movies or the way our parents' relationship was or we have some other imaginary criteria of what a good relationship looks like. We hear from women that they can't understand why their husbands won't bring them flowers, or get them cards or presents for their birthdays or Christmas. When we talk to their partners, their answer is always something along the lines of, "I can never do it right; whatever I gave her wasn't appreciated, so I have given up trying" or "We were fighting and not speaking to each other at the time." You can see there's no winning for anybody in these situations, unless you see how your thinking is creating your disappointment.

## Alison

Alison did not realize that her expectations of Simon, her husband, created a no-win situation. In therapy sessions, it became apparent that her expectations were actually met on several occasions, but her preconceived notion that Simon had little interest in pleasing her caused her to assume he fell short. In fact, she'd missed some of his positive actions! In one instance, Alison had the notion that he wasn't interested in having her family over, so when she asked if she should invite them for Easter, although he had no problem with that, she heard hesitation. She later accused Simon of behaving in an antisocial manner because he remained on the couch watching TV when they came over.

This is what came out in the session: Simon said, "Wait a minute, didn't you see that I got up from the couch to shake your father's hand and hug your mother and sister, and then when they walked to the kitchen to say hello to you, only four or five minutes went by until your father came back to the living room to talk with me." Alison had no rebuttal. She thought for a moment and realized that he was probably correct. Only a few minutes had passed. The problem was that she held a grudge that dated back about a year and half earlier. This grudge colored everything to the point where Alison found fault whenever possible, sort of like payback, except the person she was harming most was herself.

## *Reflection*

Alison was not aware that her thoughts were literally creating what she was seeing. She was reading into what Simon was doing, and that seemed real to her. She determined his motives and then used that thinking to analyze the situation. But everything was tainted and distorted by the memories she had been carrying about him through time. It is mystifying because our thinking looks so real to us at the time.

# Chapter 14

# Contaminating Our Well-being

*As our consciousness descends, we lose our feelings of love
and understanding, and experience a world of emptiness,
bewilderment and despair.*
*As our consciousness ascends, we regain purity of thoughts
and, in turn, regain our feelings of love and understanding.
Mental health lies within the consciousness of all human
beings but is shrouded and held prisoner by our own
erroneous thoughts.*
*This is why we must look past our contaminated thoughts
to find the purity and wisdom that lies inside our own
consciousness.*

–Sydney Banks

## Rachel

I love my stepdad, and I'm grateful for all he's done for me. However, I always wondered who my biological father was. I had many questions that would gnaw away at me, but my mother was unable to answer them. Finally, I decided to locate my biological father. He had been living in the next state about an hour away. I made phone contact and learned that he did not even know I existed because he and my mother had parted before she knew she was pregnant. I was grateful to hear his delight to discover that he had a daughter so close by. He immediately invited me to visit him. He was married and had a son who was about fifteen years younger than me. He told me that I was welcome to meet my brother at another time, but he was eager to meet me as soon as possible.

I had consulted with my husband throughout this process, and when he learned of my success in finding my father and that a meeting had been arranged, he was as pleased as could be. But I did not share in his excitement. I was frightened, and I conjured up every imaginable negative possibility. However, the meeting turned out to be delightful, and I had a lovely time with a nice person who welcomed me warmly.

My father wanted his wife and son to meet me. They arranged a visit with me and my husband for the following weekend. I was a mess the day before the visit with all sorts of fears and worries. I thought, "What if his wife doesn't like me; what if she finds a dust bunny or hates my cooking?"

## *Reflection*

You can see that Rachel got into an insecure state of mind. With each thought, she became more insecure. Her thoughts made it appear as though something bad was going to happen, so she continued to try to figure out how to handle these possibilities.

Rachel thought about all the things that might impact this new family's opinion of her and, of course, it looked real to her because that's what Consciousness does—it makes what we think appear to be reality. Without an understanding of the Principles, Rachel innocently contaminated her mental well-being with fearful, negative and insecure thoughts.

Worry is a way of trying to control the unknown. People innocently try to figure out what could happen in the future, thinking their predictions will help them prevent it, handle it or control it. What they don't realize is that they're just making it up in the moment, so those things might never happen.

People who worry a lot believe they have no choice. Whatever they think appears to be real, and whenever they are in an insecure state of mind, they create worries that appear real and urgent.

Remember, the content of your thinking changes with your level of Consciousness. When your level of Consciousness shifts into an insecure mode, the content of your thoughts creates more insecurity. People never worry about how wonderful their lives are or about what positive things might happen in the future.

> I've had many problems in life, most of which never happened.
>
> –MARK TWAIN

Typically, what unfolds in the present is nothing we could even have dreamed up. It's usually a surprise. That is one of the joys of life, never knowing what the next moment will bring. The unknown is interesting and exciting. Why muck it up believing in scary thoughts, unless you are making a movie in the hopes that it will become a box office hit and the next best thing to a Stephen King movie.

The best way to be prepared for something difficult in your future is to be focused in the present so you can see what's happening, and then, in a clear mind your thinking will lead you appropriately. Wisdom will always help you handle things with common sense no matter what comes your way. There is only one true antidote to our fearful imagination and that is recognizing how the Principles create our experience moment to moment.

## Deirdre and Max

I'm reminded of a counseling session with a couple, Deirdre and Max. Max said, "I realized that my worry-thinking made everything look suspect! That type of thinking makes it appear as though things external to my own thoughts have to be dealt with, changed or somehow controlled, when in fact that's just trying to change something that was created by my own thinking."

Max realized that his worry was caused by his ability to bring thoughts to life. He realized that his state of mind resets automatically. Thinking always shifts, and therefore experience always shifts.

## *Reflection*

Our thoughts come and go. When we leave our thoughts alone and allow them to pass, new thoughts automatically come to mind. Simply realizing that fact opens us up to a fresh perspective. Trying to change something you've already created is just more thinking, so you will probably start to feel frustrated and hopeless.

We are so lucky to be built in a way that allows us to recognize when we're in an insecure state of mind. If we can learn to listen to the feeling we're in, we realize we don't have to respond from that state of mind. We can then decide whether to respond or not. When we have presence of mind, in the moment, uncontaminated with past or conditioned thinking, we can know it's possible to avoid reacting. We instinctively know when to back off if we just learn to listen to what comes to us from our wisdom, which is deeper and quieter than our personal thinking. However, wisdom will not give you direction and tell you how to live your life. Wisdom simply provides you with the best vantage point from which to survey your life.

Our thinking is always changing. We always have an opportunity to wait for a better thought, one that we can trust. We can feel it. When we are aware that feelings are a guide, we see that we can stay out of the quicksand of our own personal thinking. We do this automatically whenever we don't hang on to our negative thoughts. We're making space for a better experience in the next moment. The shift happens on its own; we don't have to try to make something happen. The sooner we catch on to the way our thinking works, the sooner we are on our way to living in a better state of mind.

## Christine.

When I was in college, a burglar assaulted me. Whenever I moved into a new home, I felt vulnerable and I would get fearful, thinking and imagining someone in the house or outside the house. I lived in terror until I learned how Consciousness made my thoughts seem real. But even after I started to see how things worked with my fear, I would still have times when my husband went on his business trips and I was home alone, and those thoughts would revisit me. The last time this happened, I was in bed with my two dogs when I heard someone walking upstairs. I was gripped with terror; my heart started pounding; I was sweating and frozen with fear. I looked at my Pomeranians who were still sleeping like babies, and I remember thinking that was odd… Then a soft, little thought came in and said, "There's no second floor in this house." I started laughing, then listened and wondered what I was hearing. I realized I was hearing the sound of my own heartbeat!"

# *Reflection*

When we have a negative or insecure thought, Consciousness breathes life into it and makes that thought look and feel real. We can scare ourselves half to death. We've all had experiences where we get scared over nothing. This is an example of how the past revisits us from time to time and is recreated in such a way that it seems real again. This kind of thinking might play out in a relationship because a previous partner cheated on you, and you are insecure about the same thing happening again. You may see or hear things that just aren't there. Chris was making up the entire scary experience in her head but didn't see it at first. She was reacting to her thinking, not to an actual burglar.

## Valda and Keith

**Keith:** I remember a clear distinction in our marriage. When Valda got on my side; it was like a seismic shift. It affected me tremendously because I had been so insecure. This happened after we heard about the Principles. Up until that point, Valda had always kind of frightened me. I loved her, but she frightened me. I felt like I was almost near the edge where I could have been pushed over. There was a way Valda had about her; it was a tone that would scare me. There was a point when we both changed, shortly after we were learning about the Principles. I remember having the thought, *She's not going to leave,* and I just settled down and became so much better after that. Then I began to speak up to her, and I was less inhibited, less in my head about what to say. I got more secure and more comfortable. That shift really brought us so much closer together. It was a shift that happened on its own as we were learning more about how the Principles work.

## *Reflection*

Valda was always on Keith's side. He just couldn't see it until he had a shift in his thinking. He thought it was her tone or some other aspect about her, but really his own insecurities were interpreting her communications negatively. This is an example of how insecure thinking contaminates our well-being, and it can have a huge negative impact on a relationship. We can think something that is completely non-existent or in error, yet it still appears right to the thinker!

If you know the culprit is in you rather than in them, you can do something about it. However, if you think it's their fault or they're making you feel a certain way, there's nowhere to go but down. When we understand how our own thinking creates reality, we're less attached to the momentary appearance of life. We look at our feeling as an indication of our state of mind rather than as confirmation of the truth about the content of what we're thinking. It's much easier then to move forward in a peaceful, loving manner because we know it's a temporary trick of our personal mind.

Whether we are worrying or thinking negatively, we're being tricked by our thoughts in the moment. Remember that the bad feeling you get from negative, insecure thought or worry is only there to alert you that your state of mind has shifted, and you need to let go of that thinking and let your mind quiet.

These ways of thinking don't come from your so-called "personality"; they are just habitual ways of thinking. It's not "the way you are." It's not fixed. It's just your thinking in the moment, and that thinking changes from moment to moment and from thought to thought. What matters is the thinking we believe in and buy into.

Chapter 15

# What About the Really Bad Things

## *Health Issues*

*Life is like any other contact sport. You may encounter
hardships of one sort or another. Wise people find
happiness not in the absence of such hardships, but in their
ability to understand them when they occur.*

–Sydney Banks

### Gabriela and Will

**Gabriela:** All of a sudden, the game changed. We learned that
Will needed a heart valve replacement; open-heart surgery was on
the horizon. When I first heard the doctor give us the diagnosis,
what I really heard was, "You are going to lose him." I became
frightened and very sad. We were enjoying each other so much;
our relationship was beautiful. I instantly started preparing myself
for loss and suffering. I was grieving already. I played many sce-
narios in my mind that were based on the suffering that I saw my
mother and others experience, and I thought suffering was inevitable. I braced myself for the worst.

Will decided to retire, and I decided to quit my full-time job.
We wanted to share as much of our time together as possible. Dur-
ing this period of time we reached a new level of intimacy and joy.
I developed a great sense of gratitude for our relationship, for him

and for the present. About a year later, I started to feel really anxious again. I was confused because things were going really well.

One morning I had an insight that when I thought everything was going really well, I assumed that something really bad would follow. I thought that the better things went, the worse they were going to get later on. When I looked at my life, it seemed like the TRUTH.

I realized that my perception made life look as if I had to be in a constant state of hyper-vigilance. This way of looking at life made me afraid to love freely and to experience high levels of happiness.

I was so grateful to see this as it allowed me to be more present and to love as I pleased. I noticed that I was not holding back or pulling away. Seeing this "truth" as a thought allowed me to be free. The time for the surgery got closer and closer, and we were talking about lots of intense medical stuff. I experienced worry and stress, especially when we were in and out of the hospital. But most importantly, I felt flooded with love and so close to Will.

One of the times when we were in the hospital, they were going to perform a procedure that we had not experienced before. There were many staff in the room, and I decided to leave so I would not be in the way. I got close to him to kiss him, exchanged a few tender words, and for a moment our souls joined. Everyone else disappeared.

When I left the room, everything changed. I felt sad, worried, concerned and completely disoriented. I couldn't figure out what direction to walk towards. I was lost. What would I do without him. My world was caving in. I went from a deep feeling of love, gratitude and appreciation to complete darkness. I was walking down the hallway not knowing where I was going. I remember walking in one direction and then turning around to go in the other direction a few times. During my last turn, I heard the following, "You were born capable of being happy. You were a complete human being before you met Will." I sat down, put my head between my hands and started to cry.

We went home that evening, Will with a regular heartbeat, and I with a new understanding about life that sustains me to this day.

## *Reflection*

Death and illness seem like things that don't look like Thought. They are events that cause major emotional upheaval for most of us. You can see how Gabriela was able to go deeper in her own level of mental well-being even in the middle of a crisis. Her awareness of deeper wisdom and love helped her move to a place of gratitude. Her insecurity lost the hold it had on her, and she was filled with a positive feeling. Her ability to understand where her experience was coming from allowed her to regain her balance even while not knowing what would happen in the future.

Worry is a way of thinking about the future or the past when we're insecure. We often worry about things that are out of our hands as an attempt to control our fear. However, when we recognize that fear is coming from our own thinking, then we can make an adjustment and bring our focus back to the here and now, and wait for the insecurity to pass. We're much more likely to find a solution to things when we're in a more secure state of mind. Trying to get your emotional balance by using the same thinking that's creating the insecurity *won't* help you or the situation. If you're afraid of something that hasn't happened yet, you'll see that preparing for that event won't help if something else happens that you hadn't even thought of as a possibility. However, if you're in the present moment, just breathing or listening to another person, and something difficult occurs in that moment, you would see how to handle it in the most efficient or effective way. That's what we call hearing deeper wisdom. We always feel safe if we stay in the moment and are okay with not knowing what the future holds. Trust your wisdom in the moment.

# *Domestic Violence*

*It is a misconception to think that if you forgive someone who has harmed you, you are somehow condoning their behavior, making yourself vulnerable so that you will allow them to repeat their hurtful action.*

–SYDNEY BANKS

## Joe

As I sat there, listening quietly to Vince, a man who repeatedly hurt his wife, what occurred to me to say astounded me. I said, "I bet you that there's nobody in your life, no one in your family, in the sheriff's department, police departments, your friends, nobody in your life who hates domestic violence the way you do." Vince was talking over me at that point…then he stopped. He looked at me and said, "What did you just say?" I said it again. As I said it, he began to tear up, and he paused. Then I stopped for a moment, in silence, and he said, "How did you know that?" I said, "I don't know. I just heard that underneath what you were saying," and then we talked for a good two hours probably. He talked about his history. He experienced domestic violence when he was in his own family with his father and his mother, and he had no real history of long relationships. He didn't talk about the love that he had for this woman, he just talked about his life. Towards the end, we just talked about what true peace is and what can happen in life knowing that.

I spoke to him about how Thought works to give us an illusion of reality, and I gave him a set of tapes on the Three Principles and Domestic Violence.

After his two-year prison term, Vince showed up in my waiting room to return the tapes. Since I had some time, we talked a bit. This man had really changed. While he was in prison, Vince and his wife, Sara, were in a writing relationship, and he said that was really helpful because he was able to "listen" to her that way. He said they had some phone conversations, and they realized they just really don't do well together. They both recognized that and got divorced.

After he left I called a buddy of mine at the prison to ask him if he knew Vince. He said, "Yes, I know him, absolutely. He did really well and even taught a domestic violence course here—he used a set of tapes."

I said "Really? How was his course received?"

"It was received very well. We had a lot of people who came back and said it was great."

I looked in the tape box, and I saw that the cassettes were all white and worn out; he'd really used them. I just chuckled when I saw that. Vince had got something very, very deep. He was a different person after he saw the truth behind his state of mind, the truth behind the Principles, in a profound way that changed his life.

## Reflection

You may be thinking that there are some things that are not created by your thoughts, that some things happen in the world that affect us no matter how much we understand the Principles. Things happen in the world, such as domestic violence, because of the low level of Consciousness of many people.

When people understand how Thought works, they're able to see their own innocence and the innocence of others. They understand they were caught up in their insecure thinking from the past, and they are set free. When this shift happens, they recognize that being caught up in their own thinking may hurt people, even though that wasn't their intention. This is how you can tell if people actually change. They have to know that their behavior was coming from them, not from another person's behaviors. A shift in their understanding has to occur, where they see that their experience of life is created from within. Without this shift in understanding, no matter how remorseful and apologetic they may be in the moment, the change will never last. A shift in their understanding will result in them realizing that no one else is controlling their thoughts, emotions and behaviors. Not only would they be remorseful and apologetic, but they would also be different across the board.

It's important to grasp this point: Understanding innocence does not mean that people are not responsible for their bad behavior. Rather, they understand what is behind their behavior and the behavior of other people. A shift in perception allows people to take control of their emotional reactivity and their behavior. They then see that their thought is creating their experience, which allows them to stop blaming everyone else for the fact that they are out of control. When we think that other people are the cause of our negative emotions, we become blaming and reactive. When perpetrators of violence begin to see that their thinking causes their reactivity, they realize they need to change themselves, not the relationship.

As a person's consciousness rises, their behaviors naturally become more positive, and they begin to see things within themselves that had been in their blind spot when they were in lower levels of Consciousness.

The reason people enter counseling to change a relationship is because they are caught in the illusion of their own thinking. It really looks to him that if she made turkey instead of ham, he wouldn't have a reason to get so angry. When someone doesn't understand that their feelings are coming from their own thinking, they can easily be tricked into doing something hurtful to their partner.

In most couples' minds the notion of changing a relationship entails getting the other person to change. Ninety-nine percent of the couples who come to us think they have problems in their relationship because of what their spouse is doing wrong. In fact, a colleague of ours, Louie Pavao, found a way to guarantee attendance in his domestic violence group when he chose a topic for the evening, calling it "How to Change Your Wife." Everyone showed up, anxious to hear tips on how to change their wives. We're not making this up.

In these groups, Louie would talk about how they needed to change their level of Consciousness as a way to change their life because it would change their perspective about their wives. Once their level of Consciousness rose, their perceptions of their wives changed and they saw their wives through new eyes. Once their level of Consciousness rose, their life seemed to change, and they started to look within themselves.

When the individuals in the relationship focus on themselves, change in the relationship occurs automatically. As people let go of their negative thinking about the other person, their experience changes, and it appears as though the other person has changed. A subtle shift in your understanding can make a huge shift in the quality of your relationship.

We also work with people who have been victimized by their partner's behavior, impacting either their mental or physical health. When we talk to them about how the Principles create our experience and that learning about them will help, they typically look at us as if we're crazy or in denial!

Please know, we would never say that anyone should sacrifice their safety to save their relationship. Living in fear because you are too insecure to leave a relationship is not healthy thinking.

## Helen

I grew up in domestic violence as a child and was in a violent relationship with my partner. I've been married five times. The first marriage that I had was physically abusive. One thing that I did notice was that all of them, except my last two, were abusive, but none of them had the same pattern of abuse. I thought that domestic violence was just physical abuse. I was only seventeen when I married my first husband right out of high school, and he was physically abusive. He was a heroin addict. I had no idea, and he was very violent when he didn't get his drugs. I got out of that marriage pretty quickly. After a few years, I met my second husband who was very loving, very kind. We had our first son, but he was a womanizer so he never hit me, but emotionally it tore me apart and that was a new kind of abuse. My third husband was verbally and emotionally abusive. One day he got physically abusive.

I said I would never stay with a man who was physically abusive because I saw my mama being abused by my dad. I ended up going to a battered women's shelter. After I started feeling better about myself, I wanted to advocate for other women so I started volunteering for the shelter. I became a spokesperson for their United Way campaign. I spoke at University of South Florida where I met an attorney; she had gone through a program based on the Three Principles. She heard me speak about the fact that I was making bad choices and that I had some stinking thinking going on. She came up to me and told me that there was a Health Realization Workshop coming up. She said, "This class will really help you," and it did. It was the class that changed my life. What I realized was that the stuff that was bothering me was only bothering me because I was living in my past thoughts! I left my third husband in 1991, and this class was in 1996! I had seen about seven psychiatrists, I was on Xanax and Tofenel, and I was still just as miserable. My poor little kids. I didn't want them to laugh because sometimes they would laugh, and it sounded like a freight train was right in my head. I was so caught up in all this thinking from my past.

At one point, the facilitator of the workshop said to me, "Think of somebody you dislike." I immediately thought about my third ex-husband, and then she said, "Think about the good in that person." At that time I could not think of anything good. I just thought about the horrible names he called me. She said, "All of us have good inside; we just get caught up in our thinking." She asked me, "What do you like about him?" I had loved the fact that he was a good daddy. When I met him, he had a daughter, and he was so good to her. I wanted him to treat me like he treated his daughter. She asked, "When was the last time he did that?" and I said, "1991."

Then she stopped and said, "Really?" And I said, "Yes really." And then she said, "Honey, this is 1996." And something snapped. I was like, "Oh my gosh, five years, I've just been reliving that tape in my head about what happened to me five years ago." I wasn't living in the now; I was living in the past. It was like a ton of bricks just tumbled off my shoulders, and I thought, "I have to tell people about this understanding."

I was so excited! I had been in a mental hospital a couple of times for nervous breakdowns from just worrying about this stuff from my past, and I got into a cycle of thinking about what had happened to me. I recognized it's just Thought; it's not happening to me now. It had just become real to me because I kept thinking about it, and Consciousness kept making it real now. I saw my thoughts for what they were, that they didn't have the power that I was giving them.

I had made up my mind as a little girl that I would never let anybody beat me, but I think women stay in abusive relationships because they see another side of their partners. Everyone has a good side. Sometimes the smallest thing would trigger him, and this other side of him would come out. It's called the "honeymoon phase" when, in the beginning, they are all sweet and nice and kind. You always try to get back to that moment.

Another reason a lot of women stay in abusive relationships is because they feel threatened. Then there is the verbal abuse. I would think, "Well he didn't hit me; he was just verbal." He'd always say ugly things and be angry but never physically abuse me, so I would stay with him longer because he wasn't hitting me. I thought abuse was just hitting. I didn't realize that name-calling and cursing me out was emotional abuse. Here I was holding onto all the stuff, taking Xanax and seeing a psychologist, all because of the things he said to me in the past. I see why women stay with abusers. They don't know they're being abused, or they don't think they can do better or make it on their own. I was just looking for someone to love me.

## Reflection

Many people in dangerous situations do not even realize how much danger they are in at the time. Their positive thinking—*he loves me; he is not like that all the time; she's under a lot of stress;* and so on—or their negative thinking—*no one else would want me; I don't deserve anything more than this; it is my fault; I can't make it on my own*—will keep people from properly assessing their situation. Frequently, people distort things in a way that makes the situation look better than it really is.

Excessive alcohol and drug use, gambling and any kind of violence are signs that a person is in a low state of mind and is not aware that their thoughts are creating their experience of life. They frequently believe that they must have control of the outside world, i.e. a spouse or a partner, in order to feel more secure on the inside. The illusion of Thought works in such a way that it can appear as if their partner is responsible for their good feeling. When the good feeling passes and they begin to get caught up in more insecure negative thinking, it appears as though the insecurity must come from the other person. Over time, people in these kinds of relationships frequently believe their partner's negative or hurtful words about them are true. They begin to think that maybe the abuse is their fault because they're equally caught up in their own insecurity, making it appear as though their partner's words about them are actually real and accurate. As a person understands how the Principles work, they can quiet down to access common-sense thinking that will guide them toward safety. Then they will realize they are not making their partner feel anything. Remember, it's the Principles of Thought, Mind and Consciousness at work, making them feel everything.

The abusing person often promises to change, and they really want to change in that moment. Their desire to change typically comes from their own fear that they will lose their partner because they're dependent on them.

The desire to change must come from *insight*, not from insecurity. A deep enough insight will transform a person. They would not just be sorry for their behavior; they would become different inside themselves. Unless they see deeply within themselves that their experiences are always coming from their thinking, no matter how much they want to change, the change will not be permanent.

The most important thing to remember is that a person is not in a healthy state of mind if they are obsessed with you, control everything you do, intimidate you, hit you, rape you or do anything to hurt you. These behaviors come from an insecure perception of life. Sometimes it may not look to you like they are insecure because they act as though they are in charge and seem secure within themselves. It's easy to misinterpret controlling self-righteous behavior as security; but in a secure state of mind, they would never hurt or try to control anyone else.

## Addictions: Looking For Relief In All The Wrong Places

*When the desires of your mind trouble your spirit, your life becomes turmoil. My advice is to learn to free yourself from too many desires.*

–SYDNEY BANKS

### Cathy

Cathy, a bright, talented, creative, energetic woman, initially came to me for help with her relationship. She also wanted to understand her alcohol binges and "be done with them for the last time." She realized that she could go for months, even years without a problem, even have a drink or two here and there with dinner or with friends, and then unexpectedly wind up going out of control and be back in detox. It hardly made sense until she shared her story.

Apparently, Cathy had a million and two things she wanted to accomplish every day. Aside from a demanding full-time job, she loved to practice piano and sing, she loved reading, cooking and exercising, and the list went on and on. She would fulfill all of these desires along with high expectations of herself, burning the candle at both ends until the candle burned out. She realized that alcohol was her escape valve. Suddenly, she realized that she had made alcohol her one excuse to stop all activity. She said,

"The irony is that it was the one thing I thought I could control in my life, but inevitably I would lose control of it."

Cathy began to realize that she could "lose control" without the help of alcohol. Simply reading by the fire was a great way to escape the demands she placed upon herself. She also began to realize that the demands of her job were self-inflicted. We all have the capacity to lighten up on ourselves and retain the right amount of responsibility to meet our obligations. It is a matter of putting one foot in front of the other, staying in the moment and trusting in our innate health to take the focus off our unhealthy personal thoughts.

Cathy's job required a lot of travel. She lost a lot of sleep worrying that she might miss her flight. This was because of one instance many years earlier when she did miss her flight. It happened after 9/11, and the new rules went into effect about the size and number of bags brought on board the plane. At the last minute, she was told she had to check a bag, which caused her to miss the flight as well as the first day of meetings at her destination. Even though many business travelers ran into the same sort of thing and wound up missing meetings as a result, Cathy never let go of her experience. That one difficult day stuck with her for years so that she used her ability to think as an excuse for worry. It fit into her pattern of holding herself up to unreasonable expectations. Once she recognized that she knew how to pack for trips, there was no reason to worry—it was unproductive, served no purpose and only resulted in lost sleep—her experience shifted.

Cathy became interested in how her thinking resulted in nonproductive, even harmful outcomes. She became more interested in the source of her experience (her ability to create experience via Mind, Thought and Consciousness) rather than focusing on the *content* of her thoughts. The shift in thinking resulted in less attention to the thoughts that told her to have a glass of wine to unwind and allowed healthier thoughts to come to mind instead. As a result, she began to appreciate herself more. She had seen first-hand how easy it is to follow unhealthy thoughts when you don't realize that you made them up to begin with, and you can just as easily wait for a better thought to emerge. A side effect of learning more about the effect Cathy's thinking had on her well-being was that she became more patient with her partner.

## Reflection

Addictions are just an individual's way of trying to feel better. When we don't know that feeling better comes from within, it appears that things providing temporary relief and temporary good feelings are a person's best shot to get relief from their stress. They live in a state of stress, and on one level, they know they could live in a better state of mind. They just don't see how they can go directly to a state of innate mental well-being. It appears as though the answer is to find something in the outside world to give them relief from their problems and stop their negative thinking.

In order for something to become addictive, the individual must see it as a way to feel better when they are feeling stressed and insecure. In other words, they would have to have a momentary experience that seemed to make them feel better or different. People can get addicted to almost anything—reading books, heroin, violence, risky behavior, sex, gambling and many other unhealthy behaviors.

Generally, gamblers want the high of "hitting the jackpot" or "paying off their debts." Alcoholics want to feel more social or secure, or to quiet their thoughts. Sex addicts are thrilled by risky behavior, wanting to feel loved and desired. It's all quite innocent. People become innocently caught up in harmful behaviors because they don't understand the connection between their state of mind and their experience. The thoughts that feel urgent (what people refer to as urges) are just thoughts being brought to life by Consciousness. After a while, people frequently say they didn't even have a thought, they just acted as though they were on automatic pilot. When a person knows that "urges" are just thoughts being brought to life, they are less gripped by those thoughts, and they are able to calm down and redirect themselves. It truly is that simple, for those who *SEE* it.

People will look outside themselves for relief from their stress when they don't realize that stress is the product of their state of mind. All they have to do is recognize that fact, and then their mind will settle down on its own. When people look outside themselves to relieve their tension, they may find temporary relief from their problems, but over time those problems only worsen.

Whether using alcohol, drugs, gambling, sex, pornography or any other harmful behavior, the addiction absorbs the mind so that nothing else can enter a person's Consciousness. All of these distractions only work for a while, and like any technique, the person using them has to up the ante. This is why people have multiple affairs, why they increase the dangerous exploration of sexual activity, why they have multiple addictions and why their drug and alcohol use increases over time.

An addiction is not good for your relationship because your attention is on your addiction rather than on relating to the people you love. The negative consequences of poor judgment can cause financial problems, affairs, physical problems and more. The illusion of Thought can trick you, and you won't see that *you* are creating these problems. This is what people refer to as denial.

When a person is insecure, there is nothing outside themselves that can ever satisfy them. Since they are really looking for internal satisfaction, no drug or sexual contact will ever be enough. They're not getting a deeper feeling of well-being; they're just getting a feeling of excitement.

In the final section, we'll talk more about how to find that deeper feeling of internal well-being, but for now let's explore some aspects of various addictions.

# Gambling

## Aaron and Heather

Aaron and Heather came to see me for relationship problems that they thought were created from blending their two families. The couple had two children together and had recently gained custody of Aaron's two older children together from a previous marriage. The stress and strain of Heather's thinking about the additional responsibility caused her a great deal of insecurity and prompted many arguments.

In about the third session, it came to light that Heather had a problem with gambling. She denied it, but Aaron said it worried him greatly and caused him to judge her as being irresponsible even though she was highly responsible in all other areas of her life.

After a few more sessions and reading some books on the Principles, Heather realized that the only reason she gambled was to get out of the house. She didn't even like doing it, but it was the only thing she could think of to get some space from the four children wanting her attention so much of the time. Once she realized that she had been using gambling as an excuse to get away, it no longer had a hold on her. In fact, she realized she could let Aaron know when she needed some time alone. Taking a break helped her be a better parent because she'd return from her time alone refreshed and able to have more patience with the children. Heather stopped gambling altogether. It had lost its appeal once she saw how she was using it.

## *Reflection*

You can see how this person got hooked on something in order to find relief from stress. Heather was already thinking that her stress was coming from the outside—her family. When she found relief from something outside herself, in this case, gambling, she wanted to do it more and more, and eventually, she felt as though she had even less control.

When people find positive feelings while they are doing an activity, they often automatically attribute the positive feeling to what they are doing in the moment, without an understanding of the inside-out nature of their experience. It's fun to spend a hundred dollars in a casino and then think of it as entertainment for the evening as long as you go home after you've spent the hundred dollars. But some people get caught up in the thought that they're going to win and that one more time will do it...just one more time. Others get caught up in gambling simply in trying to pay their mortgage or their credit card bill. Before they know it, they start thinking how easy it is to pay their debts off, and they get hooked.

# Pornography

## Mary and John

Mary and John were married about five years when they came in for marriage counseling. Mary reported that John spent an inordinate amount of time in the basement "working." His computer was down there, and he disappeared for hours at night after dinner and also on the weekends. He stopped spending time with his buddies and spent almost no time with his children. He also lost interest in being intimate with his wife. She felt that something was wrong but didn't know what it was. Mary thought he was having an affair and was talking to the person online. One day she was home from work caring for one of their children, and she decided to go down into the basement to see what he was really doing. She opened up his computer and was shocked to see that he had been watching dozens of porn sites. She demanded that they go to counseling, and that is why they came in.

Mary felt that John had cheated on her even though he assured her that he had never cheated in person. Even though everything he did was virtual, she said she could tell when it started because he had changed. He was less interested in her sexually, never initiated sex anymore, was preoccupied a lot when he was with the family and he was also more short-tempered and impatient with the children. She also felt sick to think that her husband was watching young people who were probably victims of sex trafficking or only saw themselves as being good enough to perform pornographically for a living. She felt inadequate to compete with the images he saw on the screen.

John was caught red-handed and confessed to what he had been doing. He said he knew it was not healthy, but he thought of it as a stress reducer. He was tense and anxious when doing his work and used pornography as a short-term stress management technique. Over time, he spent more time managing his stress than he did working. He said he would go downstairs, and it was so easy and seductive that he found himself getting lost in the images and his own thinking about what he was looking at online.

John really wanted to stop, and Mary was open to forgiving him. They both wanted to stay married, so they were open to learning how to live in healthier states of mind. Mary realized that her intuitive thinking had directed her to snoop and uncover the secret. This helped her to feel secure that she would know if anything started up again. She also realized that his behavior was not about her. She saw how he innocently got caught up in watching pornography as a way to deal with the stress he felt as a father, husband and provider. She also developed compassion for John, yet was clear that the behavior had to stop. They both started to quiet down and focus on living in a more beautiful feeling at home. John stopped working so much and brought his computer upstairs. The basement became a playroom for the kids.

## Reflection

Mary and John were able to help each other stay out of negative thinking, and as a result, they began to feel closer than they had ever felt. They both said that understanding how the Principles worked helped them to change.

They were able to create a life that far surpassed their former life. As they started to see how the Principles worked within them, John's compulsive need to consume pornography dropped away, and Mary felt more secure knowing that it was not her fault.

Pornography has become a serious problem for many people. People who become addicted to porn are so used to being aroused by their own thinking that their relationships with their significant others can never compete with the illusion they get from pornography. One of the reasons that Internet porn has become such a problem with adolescents and adults is because it is so accessible and secretive. People can access it in the privacy of their own home or office without anyone knowing. People become further isolated, and the ground is then fertile for an addiction.

# Electronics

## Moana and Keali'i

Moana and Keali'i and their three teenagers were on the phone or computer almost all the time. Dinner involved everyone sitting at the table eating together while they were on their individual devices. They thought that meant they were connecting and having dinner together. Trouble started with their children. They began struggling in school. The teacher asked that one of them be evaluated for attention deficit disorder. One of them became depressed, and she became involved with a boy, or so the boy said, on the Internet. He told her that he was depressed and on antidepressant medication, and that he was cutting himself. She started to think she was depressed, began isolating herself from her friends and wanted to be put on antidepressants. Her parents wisely decided to take her to therapy instead. As the family learned about how their thinking worked, they realized they were a distracted family. They began to limit time on electronics and never allowed the use of devices when they were together as a family.

They started to notice that they all slowed down, felt less stress and felt more connected. Everyone complained at first, but it wasn't long before they realized they didn't like the feeling they got when they were so focused on their devices. They preferred having a quiet time together and talking at the dinner table. The kids started to do better in school, and the daughter ended her online relationship because she realized it wasn't real.

## *Reflection*

It doesn't matter if you are thinking about work all the time or using electronics, you will not have as deep a connection to your loved ones. Giving yourself time to allow your mind to stop processing will help you do a better job as a spouse, a parent or a co-worker.

Anything having to do with the Internet can become an addiction: video games, texting, sexting and social media can be used in ways that become destructive to their real-life relationships. We can all be easily distracted by electronics. We use social media to make us feel connected to each other on the outside. This is never as good as connecting in person. Social media sometimes feels like a lifeline to the world, but it can be a source of stress and compulsion. People become so compulsive about the information they receive that they often feel more connected to their phones and computers than they do to their families and loved ones.

In our counseling practices, we have seen a rapid increase in distracted family members. We all know that texting and cell phone use can be distracting when driving a car, but what you may not realize is how it can affect your relationships. People not only become addicted to the Internet for sexual stimulation but also for intimate conversations, information on world events or details of life. When this kind of addiction happens, people are more conscious of their devices than they are of the people they love. They begin to connect intellectually to something that seems to provide some positive feeling. Teenagers say that video games provide stress release. Social networks amplify the drama and allow connections with people all over the world. As a person spends more time involved with these distracting behaviors, they feel compelled to spend even more time doing them.

We work with couples that are so attached to their electronic devices that they communicate more by text or email than in person. The attachment to their devices often takes a toll on relationships because they are not focused on living in love with their partner. Their significant other will likely feel their absence and react to it, or both partners may be distracted and then start to think they've fallen out of love, and they have! But they can come back just by moving in the right direction, toward their partner instead of toward the addiction.

## The Commonality of All Addictions

The addictions listed here are just some examples of addictive behaviors. All addictions are really just a person's attempt to feel good when they are in an insecure state of mind. The person doesn't realize that what they are doing is simply feeding their insecurities rather than making them go away. It is the worst feeling to do something you don't really *want* to do, but you can't seem to stop yourself.

Being out of control feels bad because we're judging ourselves for doing something we don't want to be doing, and we don't understand why it's happening. We frequently draw the conclusion that we're flawed humans, and therefore, we're different from other people. It feels as though there's something wrong with us.

There's nothing wrong with you or anyone else; we just get caught up with our thoughts when we get stressed and insecure. Most people don't know how wisdom works, so they resort to their intellect for answers and wind up doing the same thing over and over expecting a different outcome. Our memory tells us to do the same thing because that's what we've innocently programmed into it. On another level, we know we're doing something that's not a good idea, which is why most people keep it a secret. This only adds to our insecure thinking, ultimately increasing the compulsion of the addiction.

With an understanding of the Principles, people can recognize why they do things that are self-sabotaging and that make them feel ashamed or guilty. Because people know they're doing something that's not healthy for them, they develop secretive behaviors. Keeping the secret fuels their insecurity, which then creates more insecurity, resulting in a greater need to use their addiction to feel better. When they go to that same level of thinking to get answers, they can only come up with the same old answers, which results in the same outcomes. The addiction spirals out of control, and the negative consequences of this state of mind validates their worst fears. When they recognize that they are not out of control and *it's just their thinking*, they can find a better state of mind internally, knowing that nothing outside themselves can supply that quieter feeling.

This limited section on addictions is just a brief overview of how to understand addictions in a relationship, but these are not the only things to which people can become addicted. Other common addictions are food, overeating or not eating; self-harming behaviors, such as cutting; even work or exercise can become addictions. Falling in love also can become an addiction for people who are fearful of true intimacy.

# *Divorce and Parenting, Step-Parenting and Co-Parenting*

*I have seen children successfully surmount the effects of an evil inheritance. That is due to purity being an inherent attribute of the soul.*

–GANDHI

## Divorce

### Kieran

I started working with a teenage boy, Kieran. His parents, Owen and Hattie, were getting a divorce, and his father wanted him to talk to someone. Kieran was the only child of that relationship, but both parents also had children from previous marriages. They were financially wealthy and were engaged in a hotly contested divorce.

Owen and Hattie were reacting to each other and putting their son in the middle of their conflict, yet neither parent could see what they were doing to him. Hattie was creating a coalition with Kieran against Owen, telling him the details of the divorce in order to get him on her side. Kieran felt protective of his mother against a perceived controlling father. Owen was insecure and controlling of both his son and his wife. Kieran thought his father was crazy and had a hard time trusting Owen because of the way he interacted with Hattie. Both parents reacted badly if Kieran contacted one parent while staying with the other parent, and they'd get angry with him if the other one received extra time. Owen and Hattie also tried to outdo the other with gifts and opportunities.

Kieran felt caught between the two parents and their separate views of reality. He frequently felt guilty because he preferred to be with his mother, but he really loved his father, too. He wanted to please both parents but couldn't because they were so negative and

139

suspicious that they were always seeing the worst in each other. The negativity was toxic for him.

He felt pressure, and it stressed him to think he'd upset either of them. If either parent expressed anger, he thought it was his fault, even if it didn't pertain to him. Kieran knew that both parents loved him, but he thought that they were angry at him when they reacted to something he told one about the other. Their suspicions and anger with each other spilled over into their conversations with him.

I met with both parents to try to see how I might help them to relax and interact with each other with less animosity and suspicion. Neither parent was making much progress, so I suggested they get an attorney to protect their son. They were using Kieran as a pawn in negotiations for the terms of their divorce. The attorney was able to intervene and get them to prioritize their son's needs and settle down.

Eventually, Owen attended a Three Principles weekend seminar and realized that he had to deal with his anger and lack of forgiveness. He calmed down and started to see that his state of mind was hurting his son and making him act like a person he didn't want to be. He wanted to fight for his son so Kieran wouldn't think Owen had abandoned him as his father had done to him. But in doing so he was creating the perception that money was more important than his son. Owen started living in more positive feelings, and Kieran said that he noticed it right away. Gradually, Owen was able to forgive Hattie, and he realized that he had contributed to the negativity in their relationship. He agreed to do whatever the court thought was right; he just wanted his son to be happy and psychologically healthy. As he changed and became more secure, Owen was able to see that the fight with Hattie was killing his feeling of love and replacing it with insecurity and anger.

# *Reflection*

As Owen became healthier, he was able to parent his son without getting angry. He realized that he had to work on himself and saw how that would also help Kieran. He realized that there would be life after divorce and that he would need emotional stability to start his life over again. This was so important for both his son and himself. As Owen calmed down, Kieran started to feel happier, catch up in school, stop being so attached to his phone or involved in the problems of his friends.

In general, divorce is the result of negative thinking, and it really appears as though your spouse is someone you can no longer live with for a variety of reasons. What people don't see is that these reasons are just thoughts in their own minds. When children are involved, no matter how amicable the divorce, the children tend to feel insecure. In this case, Owen was always waiting for Hattie to change so he could stop defending his position. He thought if he gave in she would take advantage of him, and his son would think the fight was all about money and not about him. His thinking came from his personal insecurity. He had never felt good about himself, so he relied on his money for his self-esteem. When Hattie had an affair and left him, Owen was extremely hurt. He became controlling without even realizing it; he just thought he was reacting to the evil force (his wife) that was attacking him. It didn't look like control to him because he didn't see how insecure he was. He thought Hattie was making him feel insecure, and therefore, making him react the way he did.

You may find it interesting that parenting comes next in this section on "things that don't look like Thought." We believe it belongs here because parents are easily tricked by their insecure thinking with regard to their children. They tend to be blind to how their own insecure thoughts and behaviors negatively impact their children. It's also easy for parents to personalize their children's behavior. Parents frequently react to their children's inappropriate behavior as if it's a reflection of their ability to parent effectively.

Think back to the section on separate realities and relationships earlier in the book. These same ideas apply to parenting. We find that people seldom agree on ideas about parenting. It's easy to judge your partner's parenting style as wrong or inadequate compared with your own style. Our individual style of parenting will be based on what we observed from our own parents and what they learned from their parents. Let's face it; none of us had perfect teachers. The best teacher for any of us is our own wisdom. If you go inside yourself, get quiet and find a loving feeling, you'll be well on your way to using wisdom and common sense to be the best parent you can be.

We think there are four basic ingredients to good parenting: To be secure, present, calm and loving. In a secure state of mind, parents know how to interact with their child. It's automatic. In a calm, present state, parents use discipline as a means of teaching, not to punish. Punishment is not a good motivator. When you are present in the moment, you'll see your children with fresh eyes, not as they were when they were five, throwing tantrums, and not even how they were yesterday. Not seeing your children as they are in the moment will only mar your clarity, and they will likely react with anger. Always have your eye on their innate health. It's always there.

You won't have to teach them how to get into a state of innate mental health; they'll be there automatically when they feel secure and calm. All you need to do is guide them back gently—it's a natural state of mind. Guide them and educate them about how the Principles work so they grow up in a state of mental well-being, unaffected by insecure mental chatter.

Parenting teens can be especially challenging. Teenagers start to notice that they have their own thoughts, even though most don't know that's where their behavior comes from. Most teenagers think their parents don't respect them and don't listen to them. Your job is to listen calmly, try to understand how they see things and gently point them back to their wisdom. To do that, you need to step back before reacting to them and find a nicer feeling by calming down and being present.

## Parenting

### Erika

When it came to bigger things, like parenting, I found so much perspective and sensibility in the way my husband, Tim, did things.

Because it's so easy to get stuck in the "I'm-right-they're-wrong" mindset about our own ideas, I'd been dismissive of my husband's parenting. Tim would let the kids watch TV before homework sometimes, which was unheard of in my world. I'd get frustrated with him. I'd made up my mind that he was letting the kids down, and ultimately letting me down, by taking the easy road.

Just like the dishwasher situation, I took a fresh look once I stepped down from my high horse and saw that Tim valued rules and structure in parenting just like I did. I also saw that he felt the freedom to be flexible, to be lenient or easygoing about homework whenever it seemed appropriate to him. I saw how that approach had its own benefits both to his mentality as a parent and to the kids and their character development. I saw that he was often more relaxed in the way he handled the kids, relative to how I'd been, and how that was a benefit I hadn't even seen, let alone respected, up to that point.

Our differences continue to offer me a chance to wake up to the limitations, tension and struggles that manifest as the echo of my own shortsighted ideas that I carry through life. Having people around me that don't fall prey to those ideas became an incredible gift I'm only just starting to appreciate.

At the moment, when I'm irritated by Tim's ways, I know I'm being self-righteous, judgmental or dismissive, I've started to see that the source of that unpleasantness is in my thinking, not in his behavior. It's a subtle shift in my understanding of life, in my orientation to relationships, but it's meant that each of our differences represent the possibility of humility, growth and freedom for me. And that's a huge leap coming from someone who just a few years ago thought our problems would be solved if only my husband could just be more like me.

*We are always one thought away from a better experience,*
*if you can find that thought.*

–SYDNEY BANKS

# Reflection

Parenting is not for sissies. One of the major reasons for divorce in general is disagreements in parenting styles; and in fact, the divorce rate nearly doubles when people re-marry and blend their families. Everyone has different ideas about parenting. When people don't understand the Principles, they think their ideas about parenting are superior to the ideas of the other parent.

Parenting children effectively, whether biological or otherwise, has to come from a healthy state of mind. We can't say this enough. A parent who lives in a calm, positive state of mind will see the innate health in their children and see how to draw that health out of them rather than try to fix what they think is wrong with them

Arguments over parenting styles are typically the result of a high level of stress in one or both parents. When parents are anxious and busy-minded, children start to get insecure and act out. It appears to the parent that the child is making them angry and reactive, so they try to manage the child instead of getting their own balance back.

As you become more secure, you'll know what to do as a parent because your feeling will guide you. You know your children better than anyone, and as you see more and more how the Principles work within your children, as well as within yourself, you'll see how to interact with them from a beautiful feeling, which will bring out the best in them as well as in yourself.

## Bob and Christa

**Bob:** We started out with an understanding of the Three Principles even before we got married, so our children were raised in unconditional love. That is huge because our kids literally have almost no trouble with anything, no issues to deal with. Obviously as you grow up you have questions, make decisions and so on; there's ups and downs but never anything serious. And a beautiful thing is that our grandchildren are learning from their parents. It's amazing. There is such a nice feeling among all of them. We don't talk about the Three Principles. The kids, and now their families, all live in such a beautiful feeling, that honestly they stand out.

**Christa:** I think all along we consider ourselves fortunate and are very grateful. When our first son was born, I observed in this young infant child how there is pure love, wisdom and happiness, already there to be shared. We felt we were immersed in pure love.

Bob was very fun loving and an awesome dad. Little people do have free will, and you have to understand how to be in the world. Bob saw how to help, even the young child, change his mind so he could get back to happiness. So that path to happiness was well trod. It was about that underlying feeling as Bob was saying and for these boys to understand, it was never about their achievements, our love was just there. "We love you as you are. If you ever find yourself in trouble, we are there for you, whatever it may be." And it's interesting how with that real safety net, that real security, they knew they could never do anything to diminish our love for them. They went out into the world secure and happy, and able to try the things that they were curious about and have different experiences that were of interest to them. They did achieve well; however, because that's what happens when you live in that state of mind, but that wasn't what it was about.

I guess it's because we found something for ourselves, so of course, it is how we see and live in the world. Wonders never cease because we all learned that it's not about the outside; it's about the inside in life.

# *Reflection*

This is an example of what's possible when parents understand the Principles and nurture health within their children. The understanding creates a peaceful, loving environment for children to grow up in. Can you imagine what the world would be like if everyone raised their children with this understanding?

## Stepparenting

### Emma

Being a stepparent is one of the biggest challenges I have ever had. I am still humbled by the task of being loving to people who don't want it. I feel hurt when I offer to help and then get my hand slapped and accused of interfering, or when I give them gifts and never even hear if they received them. Letting it go and returning to a positive feeling no matter what they do is a lesson in the process. I think I am cured and then…wham…there it is again! Through time, it becomes easier, but still it is a challenge for me.

One of the first things I learned was that I had expectations of how my three stepsons should behave that were really different from how I was parented. For example, I would get really upset by the rate food was consumed by three adolescent males. I would prepare food and think I had everything ready for dinner only to discover that the boys had already consumed it! I would get frustrated and angry. Then I would start thinking about how I had not signed up for all of this!

I realized that I had really negative thinking and then reflected on what I was thinking to make myself feel so bad. I realized that my mother would never have scolded me for eating food…never. I realized that my expectations should be based on how I was parented, since I think my parents were good parents. So every time I got upset, I would check in, see what was off in my thinking and make adjustments. I didn't have memories of times when the boys were small and loving to rely on, so I really had to trust that if I had a negative feeling, there was something that needed to change in me. Now I feel very fortunate to be allowed to have these guys in my life, as much or as little as it might be. I try to be graceful and love them and their children as much as they will allow me. I know that I would not have survived without knowing the Principles. It really looked like it was not me…a lot! But my grounding in how the Principles create my experience would always set me right again, and I'd start over!!

# Reflection

Stepparenting is about learning to love another person's child even if they don't necessarily want to love you back, as Emma learned in her family. The difficulty occurs when you don't know it's your thought creating the bad feelings. Frequently stepparents have expectations of the children that are made up in their minds from their own experiences. Children are used to doing things the way they had been doing them when their parents were together. When a new person with different expectations and ways of doing things comes on the scene, it generally creates some degree of havoc. When people don't understand these different ways of seeing things, they tend to take them personally.

Once someone feels insecure, their thinking becomes more negative, but it looks like their life has become more negative. It may appear that the children are purposely trying to hurt the stepparent or make them feel bad. What the stepparent may not realize is that the children are responding to their own insecurities; it's not personal to the stepparent. When stepparents start to worry, they'll typically try to control the children as a way to feel more secure themselves.

During these times, stepparents begin to think it's too hard, or it's their spouse's fault, or the other parent's fault, or they think about how they're not being supported. They have to do all the work, and they're being disrespected. The behavior can manifest in many ways, but it always begins with a misunderstanding of how the Principles work within everyone.

Stepparents often have thoughts about how children should act, and they may have unrealistic expectations without even realizing it. That can also happen with biological parents. Stepfamily members have thoughts about each other that aren't based on falling in love. Falling in love with your step-child or with your stepparent requires an open mind and heart. Typically stepparents try to fix their stepchildren before they even have a rapport with them, and then they wonder why it doesn't go well. When people don't know that everyone sees things differently, they assume that the other person must be behaving in such a way just to purposely irritate them. The situation can spiral out of control quickly.

Spouses frequently feel caught in the middle between their children and their new spouse. They may grapple with who to support in disagreements, and questions of loyalty may enter their minds. Instead of choosing sides, they need to see that they are all on the same side and they will need to create a new way of interacting from love and wisdom.

# Co-parenting

## Cathy and Marco

After nearly 25 years of marriage, Marco and I found ourselves taking opposite directions in life. We had reared a daughter who was getting ready to leave for college, and we found ourselves spending very little personal time together. We were polite and friendly and supportive of each other, as we always had been, but he didn't want to do any of the things I wanted to do (slow down, simplify our lives, drop back from so many social and community obligations and take time to travel and pursue quieter interests), and I didn't want to do any of the things he wanted to do (go out frequently to parties and events, throw big parties for his custom-ers and contacts, enjoy our social standing as business and com-munity leaders, pursue even more material success, take advantage of plastic surgery to stay young looking). One afternoon, as I was driving to a Syd Banks event, Marco called me on my car phone from a Porsche dealer and asked me what color car I wanted. I told him I didn't want a Porsche. He was hurt and offended. What I really wanted was for him to come with me to the Syd Banks event. He thought that was weird. I felt that I was looking at my marriage through the wrong end of a telescope, and life as I knew it was growing smaller and smaller.

Honestly, I'm not saying I am right and he is wrong. The one thing I'm sure of is that our own thinking looks really real to us, whatever it is, and we have to respect that. We had married right out of college and enjoyed our early life together while we were young and poor and trying to get a start in life. It seemed as though his extraordinary success in business and my very different success as an entrepreneur and activist pulled us away from each other into unrelated worlds—different colleagues, different friends, increasingly different values. I felt I couldn't be the wife he wanted any more. He couldn't relate to my friends. We both came to the realization that we cared for each other, but our marriage wasn't working. We didn't look for blame or right or wrong; we looked for amicable resolution. I have to admit that, had I come to an even deeper understanding of the Principles before our divorce, I might have seen a way to work things out. But maybe not. Divorce is a decision that, if made with a clear head and a good feeling, without judgment, might be the best decision for some couples.

And thus within a few months, with no arguments and very little upheaval, with one lawyer and one accountant helping us to work things out together, we got divorced. We both loved our daughter with our whole hearts; we were committed to making this as easy for her as possible. So while she was a bit baffled by her two "nice" parents getting divorced, so different from the nasty divorces her friends talked about, she was relieved that she could relate to us both as she always had without taking sides or having to hear anything negative from either of us about the other. Her life as an independent young woman was just beginning and, thankfully, our divorce did not disrupt her trajectory.

That was years ago. Marco married again within a year of our divorce. (I actually attended his wedding with our daughter.) I have remained close to his mother and his siblings. We enjoy coming together for big family events—weddings, christenings, funerals, major holidays. We still share business interests. I consider him a fine man, who is a good friend. As far as I've ever heard from mutual friends, he considers me an admirable woman and a good friend.

Even shortly after our divorce, we could count on each other. For example, I had remained in our house. One morning, as I was trying to leave for work, the garage door malfunctioned. I could not lift the heavy door manually, and I needed to leave. I called him to ask what I should do as he had always taken responsibility for that kind of thing. He was just leaving for work as well, but he came right to the house and fixed the garage door for me. Happy to do it. He explained to me how to fix it myself if it happened again.

He and his wife adopted a baby not long after their marriage. When our daughter was tiny, he didn't have too much to do with baby care, but he became a very involved father after she started to talk and interact. So one evening, when his wife had left him home with the baby as she went out of town for a couple of days to attend a conference, he called me in a panic. The baby was crying and crying, and he didn't know what to do. He had tried feeding, changing the diaper, playing soothing music, adjusting the lights…I drove the 45 minutes to where they lived and picked the baby up to calm her down and explained to him that sometimes you have to pick them up and burp them and walk them around. He was very grateful to have the help.

Right after our divorce, he sent me a copy of Robert Frost's poem, "The Road Less Traveled," with a note that said, *I know you and I are drawn to different paths, but I am proud that we both respect our own choices and each other. Best wishes as you take the road less traveled.*

# *Reflection*

This story is a great example of the possibilities that can happen for people who decide to divorce. Remaining respectful and positive toward the other parent of the child will save you and your children from needless suffering. You may not think this is possible, but we assure you it is, with an understanding of the Principles. If it doesn't seem possible to be respectful and positive toward your ex, re-read Chapter 10 (page 84) on innocence again. The most important thing you can do for your children is to get past animosity and ill will, and realize that separate realities are not only legitimate, they are inevitable.

When people don't understand that they are creating their reality, co-parenting following a split can be challenging. For one thing, you have to deal with the person you split from for reasons that made sense to you at the time. These negative memories can cause stress and pain for years. Parents typically think it was the divorce that hurt their children, not realizing it's really the animosity and ill will they display toward the other parent that hurts the children more than anything.

If you look toward quieting down and seeing Thought for what it is, you will begin to realize that the past is no longer real so you can let it go, and you will be able to co-parent more gracefully. You will see that you don't really know all there is to know about what happened in the past. The past is just a thought now. It's not real, so let it go and start fresh.

If you are a parent going through divorce, a stepparent or a co-parent, the answer is always the same: Look for a nice feeling before you say or do anything. Remember that you and your children have the innate capacity to find a calmer, nicer state of mind. When any of us act out, we're just caught up in our own insecure thinking. Divorce affects almost everyone in a way that creates insecure feelings, so be aware that you are not the only one going through the divorce and all the changes that come as a result. The divorce can affect people long after it has taken place, so please be sensitive to those effects. And if you're thinking about divorce, check in with your state of mind and remember that Thought has the power to trick us into doing things that look like a good idea even when they're not. Follow your positive feelings, and let them guide you.

*The higher your level of consciousness, the more
understanding will be in your heart.*

–SYDNEY BANKS

# Extramarital Affairs

## Richard

I feel terrible. I have been depressed for two years or more over this. I have a wonderful family. I've been married to a really great woman, Liz, for twenty-five years. We married when we were twenty after dating since we were eighteen, so we never had the opportunity to be in a committed relationship with anyone other than each other. We don't fight; we get along very well and co-parent our children very well, but I have always felt like something was missing.

Then I met Carla, a woman at work, who made me feel like I have never felt before. If I had not discovered this feeling inside, I would never have known what I had been missing. I told Liz about it. I am a firm believer in complete honesty.

Of course, she was not happy about it, but she knew how depressed I had been, just moping around, not engaging the children, and she wanted me to be happy. So she suggested a separation so that I could explore things on my own.

Liz could not bear the thought of me making a new life with a woman I met while I was still married to her, even if we turned out to be an ideal match. Her line of thinking did not make sense to me though because I wasn't looking for someone outside of the marriage, and in fact I had no interest even after my wife gave me the green light to find someone else. I felt like I found (actually stumbled upon) the right person for me. In my mind I didn't want to leave Liz, but I wanted to explore what could be possible with Carla.

# *Reflection*

For these people, their insecure thinking played out in a way that reinforced each other's insecurities and magnified his desire for his coworker. Richard realized that he was still hanging onto resentful thoughts he had from high school at the beginning of their relationship. She had been intimate with someone else while she was dating him. It's hard to imagine that someone could still be upset about something that happened so long ago. It hadn't prevented them from sharing their life together, but Richard didn't realize that it was just his thinking delivering his negative feelings. He never regained a sense of trust, and in fact, he was having trouble trusting the new woman in his life, even though he realized he was probably pushing her away with all of his mistrustful questions.

As Richard learned about the Principles, he began to view his relationship from a different perspective. He began to realize that changing his lifestyle and his environment by moving out of the marital home was simply seeking something outside of himself to feel better on the inside. What really needed to shift was his state of mind, and that in turn changed his perspective.

As we've seen, when our thinking changes, our feelings change and then we behave differently under the influence of different thoughts. But, to reiterate, it doesn't work if you *try* to make yourself think or feel something different. We make things up in our minds through the creative process of thinking. It doesn't look like we made it up because Consciousness makes it appear real. This is why people get tricked into an affair, knowing it's the wrong thing to do but feeling as if it's right for them.

With that said, poor Richard cannot help the fact that he feels miserable staying in his marital home with his wife of twenty-five years. However, he also feels miserable about leaving his family for what he calls selfish reasons. He doesn't realize that he doesn't have to feel miserable if he could see his thinking at a deep enough level. He could fall back in love with his wife.

Liz truly wanted him to feel better. That is what we would call love and devotion, as opposed to possession. Her love for him was so deep that she wanted him to be happy, and if that meant giving up the relationship for him, she was willing to do so.

If Richard ever had a chance to fall in love with Liz again, her kindness would certainly help him. If, on the other hand, she had become angry and bitter, he might have stayed, but it wouldn't be comfortable for either of them.

The interesting part of this anecdote is that Richard began to feel insecure thinking that Carla was capable of leaving him as well. If he could do it, so could she. The situation became so uncomfortable he almost drove her away with incessant insecure questions. Because he had given up his marriage for their relationship, he began to think Carla would also give up on him. It's a common reaction for the person who was unfaithful in a marriage to begin thinking their spouse had an affair because the spouse's reaction to them becomes distant. This is an example of how you see in your life what you're thinking. That thinking colors everything because you're so aware of it, and you begin to see it everywhere.

When people see the process, (the act of creating their life through their thoughts) they see that it is not about mucking around in their outer lives, changing addresses, spouses, jobs. All that does is trade one problem for another.

People get involved in affairs because they don't understand that their experience is coming from their own thinking. Most people who've had affairs feel guilty but use their negative thoughts about themselves or their mate to excuse the affair. When people live without intimacy for whatever reason, they suddenly find themselves in a position to be reawakened to the power of connection. They report that they feel alive again, energized, sexually attracted and attractive again. They don't realize the feelings are not coming from the other person. The feelings come from their own thinking. They imbue the situation with their own thinking, i.e. "since it was so mutual and so unplanned"; "it must be our destiny"; "it was meant to be"; "I didn't know I was capable of feeling this way." All of this thinking further convinces them to continue with the affair. As they justify their attraction, they tend to make their spouse the cause: "If he'd only listened to me"; "if only he'd paid attention to me"; "if only he hadn't worked so much"; "if only she gave me as much attention as she gives the children."

Their thinking looks valid and true because they are trying to make sense of why they have these feelings for another person. Since it feels so good, they justify the affair because they don't understand why the experience happened to them in the first place.

If you find that you are unhappy in a reasonable situation, the place to look is within, at the very core of your being. That is where Mind, Thought and Consciousness are at work, creating your experience every moment of your life.

You may not jump from unhappiness to happiness right away when you look within, but you certainly will be looking in the right direction. At the very least, you will gain a degree of separation from what you are experiencing. It's like being absorbed in a movie to such a degree that your teeth clench as though you are experiencing what you are watching. Then, all of a sudden, you remember that it's just a movie.

There are certain circumstances that seem to justify extramarital affairs, whether it's illness, an accident or circumstances beyond a person's control. However, we are generally saying that having a sexual relationship outside of your primary relationship tends to be damaging and disruptive in ways you can't imagine—to both you and your significant other, not to mention the other person you're seeing.

Be aware of the consequences of an affair. You risk losing your primary relationship because he or she may not be able to handle it or may not be willing to forgive you. Don't be fooled by your body responding to your thinking; there is a strong connection between the mind and the body.

Often, when the significant other finds out about the affair, it's common for the one that strayed to lose interest in the affair because the lure was always just an illusion of the mind anyway.

Have you ever had the thought: *I love my wife, I love my husband, but I'm not in love with him or her anymore*? If you believe that to be true, you have likely been having a lot of negative thoughts about your significant other, not thinking about them at all or just thinking too much in general. This thinking is why you are not connecting. When you feel a real connection with someone else, it seems miraculous.

It's much simpler and wiser to refocus on your significant other rather than turn your life upside down, seeking solace outside of yourself, hurting the person you love and feeling shame over actions you took when you weren't in a healthy state of mind.

If you're happy on the inside and you love your spouse, it makes sense to do everything you can to fall back in love with them rather than trying to fix things on the outside. The more people look outside of themselves for something to fix what they perceive to be wrong, the busier their minds become and the more insecure they feel. Busy minds breed insecure feelings. This is the natural outcome of a mind searching for stimulation from the outside world.

> As simplistic as it sounds all positive change comes about
> by changing our thoughts because love is a positive feeling.
> Again, it is a simple change in your thoughts that can turn
> resentment to forgiveness and love. This will assist you to
> have a better marriage.
>
> –SYDNEY BANKS

## Recovering From Affairs

> When you learn to forgive those who have wronged you in
> the past, you clear your mind and bring harmony into your
> life, allowing you to see what is, instead of what isn't. What
> isn't…is life seen through distorted memories. What is…is
> life seen as it truly is now, clear of all falsehoods.
>
> –SYDNEY BANKS

## Tom and Melissa

Tom and Melissa had been married twenty-five years when they came to see me after Melissa had a brief affair. Tom was extremely upset. He felt as though his whole world had come crashing down. He said over and over again that he would never in a million years have believed it could be possible, that he had given his all to the relationship. Again and again, he said, "How could she do something like this to me?"

Melissa claimed that she had felt timid about talking to Tom about a lot of things because "he would become defensive and take everything personally." Tom immediately retorted that it was not so, that he always asked Melissa to tell him what was on her mind.

Tom was blind to his own defensiveness, so he didn't see how he was contributing to a lack of open communication. He couldn't see how his defensiveness shut down the conversation. And in trying to prove him wrong, Melissa only felt defeated.

Melissa said she could not talk to Tom about their relationship, so she found someone else to talk to. That someone else happened to be another man. That feeling of intimacy led to her feeling a strong connection with him, and so in her mind she rationalized that the physical intimacy was something over which she had no control.

# *Reflection*

People frequently seek counseling after an affair has wreaked havoc in their life. Affairs tend to be one of the most difficult things to recover from and move on from, even if you decide to get divorced. Many people think that it's impossible to recover. They wonder, "How can I stop thinking about it, and even if I could, how can I ever trust him/her again?" Making the decision to stay in or leave a relationship is a decision to make from a healthy state of mind. When people first find out about infidelity, their reaction will be based on how personally they take the revelation and how negatively they perceive it.

How people react to finding out that their partner is having an affair varies. Some people take it very personally; they're sickened by it, have an awful reaction and suffer greatly because they perceive it as a betrayal of their trust. Other people understand that it's not something they want in their relationship, but their thinking is more pragmatic, i.e. one client reported that when she found out her husband was having an affair, she said to him, "End it now, or we're getting a divorce." He did, and that was the only conversation they ever had about it. Their relationship got back on track, and now they have been married over fifty years.

On the other hand, we've had clients who were still suffering years after the divorce, harboring negative thoughts about it and unable to move on to other relationships, fearful that they couldn't trust anyone again. If this has happened to you, you need to realize that it's insecure thinking that causes pain and suffering. Love never hurts. Feeling love is always a positive experience. Feeling love is always possible no matter what has happened because love doesn't come from other people and neither does hurt. The answer is always in forgiveness, and to forgive, you really must let go of past memories.

> *Forgiveness releases you from mental anguish and pain,*
> *and all the horrible negative feelings and unforgiving*
> *mind experiences. When you learn to forgive, you see with*
> *clarity the ignorance and innocence of those who trespass*
> *against you.*
>
> —SYDNEY BANKS

## Affair-proof Your Marriage

It is important to realize that the power of really listening to one another, without judgment or the need to defend, is what creates the emotional intimacy that people yearn for. So, if you find yourself looking for that outside of your relationship, or if you suddenly wake up after you've gotten attracted to someone else, that's a signal that you've been neglecting your partner, not listening to them or in some other way contaminating your experience of them.

Another important thing to know to help affair-proof your marriage is to pay attention to your partner by being present in the moment, being kind, loving and considerate, and having each other's back. Couples typically get comfortable and complacent in their relationship. They forget to stay focused on sharing and expressing their love. Everyone wants to feel special and cherished by their partner. Making the other person feel precious and loved will go a long way to maintaining a deep connection.

Spouses often complain to us that their partner is a workaholic or they're on the phone with friends or on social media sites rather than relating to them. Just remember the simplicity of not harboring negative thoughts about your partner or yourself to ensure a good relationship.

## Section 4

# Unleash the Magic

*There are those in this world who believe miracles do not happen; I can assure such skeptics that they do, with hope and faith as beacons anything can happen.*

–Sydney Banks

*Understanding the Three Principles leads me to realize that we are all pure love. Love is always with us. For many couples, love seems to get lost. But all that has happened is a misuse of our gift of Thought. Couples get into habits of thinking about each other, like fault finding, dissatisfaction, opinions, judgments, which create the illusion that their love has been lost. But love never leaves. However, these troubling thoughts can leave, and when they do, pure love emerges. The "Honeymoon" is never over; couples just "think" it is.*

Mark Howard, PhD

# Chapter 16

# The Feeling of Love

*Your own inner beauty will increase and grow as you recognize the beauty in others. This quality may not always seem evident, but I believe you are wise enough to know that everyone has a spark of the divine spirit, which they need only allow to come forth.*

–Sydney Banks

## Gabriela

I worked for a county department of mental health and substance abuse where I often taught courses on the Principles. One day Will, a police sergeant, asked me to present at a community college. Some dealings I'd had with him in the past left me with some unfavorable thoughts about him, but I accepted the invitation nonetheless because it was part of my job description to do so.

It turned out that, unbeknownst to me at the time, Sergeant Montano had designs on me, but I was already involved in a relationship.

Several months later, out of my previous relationship, I met Will again at a county meeting. As our conversation progressed, it came to light that I had broken up with my boyfriend. With the sincerest tone, he asked if I was doing ok. "I am well," I said. "Great," he said, "Do you want to go to the movies sometime?"

Over the next few weeks we spent time at coffee shops, ethnic restaurants and some holiday parties. I had a lot of fun with him, but it was not my intention to get serious with anyone. I was not looking for a relationship, which meant I did not have any of my "love-thinking" on. I remember having a conversation and telling him that I did not want a serious relationship. In hindsight, my stance about relationships at this time of my life gave me total freedom from the many beliefs I had about love and relationships.

Time went on, and little by little, Will was the only man I was dating. We just had such a light-hearted time; it was so effortless and fluid. I had no plans, no agenda.

One day a dear friend said "It's so wonderful to see you in love." "Who's in love?" I said. "You're in love!" and she burst out laughing. "Every time you talk about him, you smile and when he calls, you're like a little girl." I said, "Oh my God, I guess I am in love!" [*laughs*]

I became a bit worried and guarded. A couple of times in our early days, I freaked out but had enough insight to know what was happening inside of me—I was having a thought attack! I had some conversations with Will, explaining what was happening. I asked him for his help. I asked him to stay calm and grounded. "I will get back to my usual self. I promise." He understood, and soon I relaxed and returned to a feeling of love.

Throughout our courtship there were moments when I restrained myself from showing Will affection because I thought this would minimize the possibility for hurt. I did not want him to know how much I enjoyed being with him, how many times a day I thought of him, how much I loved him. I was confined by my thinking to a world of concern and limitations.

In spite of all my beliefs, thoughts and ideas about the rules of love, we started to enjoy a relationship filled with love, compassion, understanding, support and joy. Sometimes I would be frightened to lose it all. Yet within my being, there was a desire to shake off the fear that kept me limited. And life got richer and fuller, and I became less afraid to love.

# *Reflection*

You can see that Gabriela's insecure thinking about love caused her trouble. The way we think of love is often misguided and misconstrued. Love sometimes gets confused with worry, dependence, possession or lust. Whether we're speaking about love for a spouse, a friend, a child or a parent, we can see how easy it is to feel bad, all in the name of love. We've all heard phrases like, "I worry about you because I love you"; "Don't be gone too long; I need you to help me"; "I can't live without you."

Gabriela was frightened by her insecure thoughts, which created a negative reaction that might have spiraled out of control had Will not remained calm and understanding. For each of them, it was their thinking leading them in a certain direction.

The love we're talking about is not possessive; it's not demanding or smothering. It's pure. Pure Consciousness is love. Pure Consciousness, before the contamination of negative thoughts, is love. This feeling resides within all of us, and we naturally access it when we're not fraught with negative thinking.

If you've ever felt love for a companion, a child, a parent, a spouse or a friend, love for life, your country or your favorite park, you know what we mean. That feeling we touch upon will grow when we nurture it. That's the feeling that is right there, readily available, if you simply quiet your mind. Suspend your judgments, analysis and comparisons. Just Be. You already are love.

Love is the feeling we get when we're smack in the moment, unburdened by negative thoughts. Thinking in a negative direction will obliterate it. Yet love will always re-emerge, like the sun, when our clouded thoughts drift away. It always does, all on its own, when we don't make our thoughts so important. We automatically find ourselves in a lighter, more peaceful state where we see each other's true innocence.

Love is portrayed in novels, movies and television from the writers' personal understanding of love and their imagination brought to the screen or the page via the gift of Thought. Some clients have said they felt excited while reading or watching romantic stories. They then compare their relationship to these imaginary stories and begin to think critically, focusing on what they don't have. This can cause a feeling of even greater disconnection, or it can become a springboard to ignite one's own relationship with more passion. The choice is always up to the individual.

The love that everyone seeks is the love that exists before our personal thinking kicks in. Love is a positive feeling, and we all have the power to point ourselves in that direction over and over again. No matter how many times we get caught up in negative thought, we can always return to love because it comes from within ourselves *before* our thinking. Love never goes anywhere; it just gets covered up with our own negative thoughts.

When we focus on the positive, we notice more about how Consciousness works. We notice other wonderful, miraculous things we would not have noticed had our minds been on the negative. We don't notice the beauty around us when we're caught up in our negative thoughts.

## Jody

We were at dinner one night, and Mike was really out of it—couldn't sit up straight, couldn't get food to his mouth, picking up food with his hands. I had to feed him, grab his hands repeatedly so he didn't knock over his glass or pull the tablecloth off the table.

A handsome young Latino couple was sitting across from us. She was all dressed up in a darling little black dress, and I was sitting there in yoga pants with no makeup, couldn't even remember if I had brushed my hair, and I was dodging disasters while trying to eat. They were speaking Spanish, and I was hoping we weren't grossing them out. They got up to leave just before we got our tab. He leaned over as he passed and said, "Have a good night." I said, "Thank you, and you too." Kind of startled and pretty much at a loss for words, I gave the waiter my credit card before he even brought me the tab because Mike was tired, and I still had to get us back to the hotel, give him a shower and then get him to bed.

The waiter said, "That couple already took care of your tab." I was stunned. I looked out the window; they were still getting into their car, so I ran outside to thank them. I knocked on his window, and he lowered it. I said, "Thank you so much. Why did you do this?"

He said, "Is that your husband?" I answered yes, and before I can say anything else she leaned over him and said, "We just hope we can be as good a couple as you are."

Having been thrown out of a restaurant just a few nights before because the manager thought Mike was drunk after he kept dropping his silverware on the floor, I returned to the restaurant in tears. Michael has a way of bringing out the best even at his worst. I love this man.

## Reflection

Michael had early onset Alzheimer's. This story is an example of how you can stay in the feeling of love as you grow older together despite problems that may arise from the aging process. She looked at her husband through the eyes of love even as his condition deteriorated. What she saw was the man she loved inside a body that wasn't cooperating any longer.

# Chapter 17

# Listen for Connection

*Words are merely a form. Listen not to words, but to that which words attempt to convey.*

–SYDNEY BANKS

## Alan and Jean

**Alan:** While listening to Jean, I noticed my own thoughts kept getting in the way. I imagined swatting at them, as if they were flies buzzing around my head. Then suddenly, something changed. It was as though the flies flew away to find another busy mind to plague while my mind quieted down. The more interested I became in what Jean had to say, the less interested I was in my own thoughts, and before I knew it I was fully with the experience that she was describing.

I began to really hear what Jean was telling me. The quieter my mind got, the more engaged I became. I could understand her feelings more clearly than I ever had in the past. Judgment never crossed my mind. It felt incredibly freeing. With no feeling of pressure to tell her what to do, there was nothing to be done. I was simply drinking in what Jean was telling me, and I could feel her experience. It felt great to be with her so solidly, no matter what she was expressing. I felt so connected to her, just in the act of listening deeply.

**Jean:** Imagine the bliss I felt when Alan quieted down and didn't try to fix, cajole or coax me away from my feelings. In the past I would think, *Can't I just have my feelings without him trying to take them away? What's so wrong with feeling bad? It won't last* *forever*. I knew that I'd live through it. For once, I felt as though he really got what I was hoping to convey.

**Alan:** I had heard the same story from Jean for months, maybe even a year. Yet I had actually never heard what she was really saying. For the first time, I understood that she was feeling degraded. I heard Jean say that she was being treated badly at work; she felt belittled and diminished. I thought she hated how unfair things were there. So I would try to help her feel better, then I would say something insensitive like, "Well, you know, life is never fair," and then wonder why she got so mad at me, and yelled, "I don't care if it's fair or not."

What Jean was trying to tell me was that she wanted to find a way to regain her dignity at work. I realized that she didn't care about fairness in the first place—it was never about that for her. I learned something new about Jean; that fairness is not something she even notices in her life even though it's really big in my life. On the other hand, Jean can't stand it when she doesn't feel respected. I haven't felt this close to Jean in a really long time. I realize now that by trying to help her I was listening to what I thought she needed, which was different from what she wanted. I now understand more about the true nature of Thought. It's quite riveting.

However, I could lapse into enormous disappointment if I let myself think it's unfortunate I didn't know about this sooner. We would have avoided so much heartache. Instead, I realize that would just be more thinking to get in the way of having a nice time with Jean now.

## *Reflection*

This is a universal experience that couples have when they begin to see how their personal thinking gets in the way of feeling connected with their partner. When you're with your partner or someone else, notice what happens within you when you're listening to them. Are you processing what they're saying, or are you just taking it in, waiting for understanding to come from within you? Are you waiting for your turn to say what you think, or are you sitting back just taking them in?

If you are listening really deeply from a quiet state of mind, you'll feel connected with the person; you'll feel empathy and compassion and respect for their world. It won't matter if you agree with it or not. When you're listening from a healthy state of mind, you're very present, and your analytical mind is quiet. Your heart will be touched by what they have to say. That is what it feels like to listen to someone with a clear mind and a desire to understand the experience of the speaker. You may actually hear something your partner might not be fully aware of.

It feels wonderful to be heard by someone who does not have their personal thinking in the way. It requires listening with a degree of purity, with no other agenda pushing its way into the listener's mind.

Frequently we hear from couples that their reason for seeking counseling is to help them with their communication problems. Usually what we find is that they are having a listening problem. Instead of listening to understand and connect, people tend to listen to be right or to argue their point of view. Mind you, we understand this is not intentional, and most people don't enjoy arguing because arguing won't draw you closer to the other person.

As human beings, we tend to listen for what *we* think the speaker is saying. We don't typically listen at a deeper level for what the speaker is trying to express. A good example of the kind of listening that connects people is what generally happens when couples first meet. They are attentive and interested in each other. They let themselves get drawn into the speaker while their own mind is quiet. They don't have any thinking about the other person yet. What happens as people get to know each other is that they start thinking they know what the other person means. Then their old personal thinking and beliefs kick in without them even realizing it!

*The ear is the avenue to the heart.*

–Voltaire

## Karen and John

Karen and John entered counseling hoping to get their relationship back on track. They married in their mid-twenties and gave birth to a child with developmental disabilities. Both were employed in high-stress upper management positions. Early in their marriage, John was offered a position in the Far East for one year that would catapult his career. With some discussion, Karen agreed that he could take the position but later confessed that she saw no other option given John's enthusiasm for the opportunity.

Karen rose to the occasion, somehow managing to maintain her career while providing care for their special needs child. Three years later, they live in the same city but in two separate houses, sharing parenting responsibilities as though they were already divorced.

Over the course of a couple of months, it became clear to John that he had behaved badly, and he was remorseful. He realized he had been immature and selfish. It never even crossed his mind how difficult it would be for Karen.

# *Reflection*

Karen and John learned how to listen to one another. Can you see that when couples listen to one another with an open heart, without judgment or defense, they will hear things they would never hear otherwise? They will learn things about themselves and their partner they could never learn if they remained focused on their personal point of view.

Karen and John had to see the innocence in one another to be able to listen openly without bias. Karen had to see that John was innocent in his immaturity. He never meant harm to Karen, but rather he was just caught up in his own story about how the job opportunity was the only thing that mattered to him. His decision was all about John. It had nothing to do with Karen. From John's vantage point, he had no other choice but to take the position.

John was able to see that his vision was clouded by his insecure thinking. When they both quieted down, they were able to come back together and save their marriage.

Since we are creative beings, we each use our individual ways of expressing ourselves that are sometimes quirky or sometimes misguided, but we're all doing the best that we can at any particular time. We're always acting based on the way things look to us in that instant. Since we behave according to how we think and feel in the moment, we are the victims or heroines of our own making. It is only when our state of mind improves that we can look back at the past and realize we've been tricked by our own thinking. That's when we say, "I knew I shouldn't have said that. I knew I shouldn't have done that." That's when we KNOW that we had better thinking, and we didn't listen to it.

We want to listen to really HEAR what the other person is saying in order to understand them and at the same time listen to our own wisdom within to provide insight. As we understand how the Principles work, we start to rely more upon listening for wisdom and common sense to guide us.

## Jack

When listening to my partner, if she is complaining about something, I want to listen for what she really needs from me right then instead of listening to what she's complaining about. Her words aren't what matter. There have been times when she's brought up a problem she's experiencing where I have jumped in with a solution. That's almost never what she needs or wants in that moment. Most often she just needs someone to listen to her and care for her and support her. If I come up with a solution, she will rebel because that's not at all what she wants. If I'm really listening to her rather than to my own thinking about what she's saying, I will hear what she really wants from me. I'm not saying I'm there all the time, but I'm there a lot more, and when we forget and revert back to old habits, we make allowances for each other.

*It's like feeling your partner's thinking.*

–Anonymous

# *Reflection*

Jack's insight about listening helped him be more present and navigate through conversations without stepping on landmines. He was able to get a feeling for his partner's state of mind and did not take her ups and downs personally. This allowed him to respond to her needs appropriately, and the feeling in the conversation remained supportive and loving.

## Christine

My middle stepson, Peter, spent eleven months in the hospital fighting leukemia. He lost his fight with the disease but not before touching everyone who was with him in a profound way. I was lucky to help him as he taught all of us the value of life. He was twenty-four when he went into the hospital. He was still very strong at that point. He endured chemo treatments and all kinds of adventures from the clergy who wanted him to deal with the fact that he was going to die, to medications that made him worse, to the emotions of family members. Yet through it all, he always exhibited a sense of humor and a strong presence. He touched the nursing staff so much that the ICU nurses presented him with a flower lei before we turned off the machines. They told him that he had brought them all back to the reason they went into nursing in the first place. For much of the time, he was on medication that only allowed him to move his eyes, yet he was so connected that we all seemed to know what he wanted. If you have ever gone through this, you will understand the power of connection that comes in silence. I can still feel it today, twenty-five years later.

# *Reflection*

During times like this, it's easy to forget that your thinking is creating your experience. Knowing how the Principles work will help you stay strong, present and loving during difficult times. By staying very present and in a feeling of love, we experience tough times in a much different way. It is a spiritual experience to allow yourself to be in a space of not knowing, to just be present and love without fear. It seemed powerful that Peter was able to communicate with the nursing staff and his family with just his eyes. There was a magical feeling of everyone being connected as we were going through the experience together.

## Rudi

My mum had cancer, not just cancer but inoperable cancer. I loved my mum as much as any son could love their mother, and the biggest fear of my life was losing her. I just could not imagine, nor tolerate, a life without her physically in it. When the oncologist gave mum the death sentence date of, "I don't think you will last beyond 10 weeks." I immediately spurred into action to "save" her. However, people have to want to be saved in order to be saved, and my mum definitely did not want to be saved!

I suggested things that would help, pleaded with her to try other approaches and argued with her to make her see "sense." All to no avail. She was quite happy with her McDonald's burger in one hand, cigarette in the other and a strong black coffee steaming on the side! Over the weeks, I watched this proud, beautiful woman wither away. The more I tried to help her, the more we disconnected. Eventually, halfway through the death sentence, I broke down in tears and cursed the gods above, or whatever was listening, for slowly taking her from us and for her unwillingness to help herself. The storm of curses, tears, anger and desperation left me feeling empty and despondent. I asked a question in my mind, *How can I help her?*

Out of the vast quietness, an answer majestically arose. It was obvious, but I had not seen it. *Just love her.* It was so simple, yet so simply profound. I got over myself, my own needs, my own fear and started to truly think of her without my own agenda. I stopped trying to get her to change or get her to think like me. We each had different thought-created beliefs, but love goes beyond beliefs. We had different thought-created opinions and "truths," but love also goes beyond opinions and is the truth behind non-conditionality. When I saw her again, I just loved her. I chuckled at her terrible (to me) eating habits and didn't frown when she got the cigarettes out. I guess she decided she was going to "kick the bucket" (as she used to joke about), so why the hell not enjoy what she enjoys?

My last five weeks with her, without forcing my own seemingly justified agenda on her, were truly miraculous. We cried together, we hugged and sometimes we would laugh so much our stomachs hurt. It is amazing what happens when you don't try to change people and drop any conditions about them being anything. People talk about wanting to "connect more with others. Well, connection is just another word for no separation. It's what naturally happens when you are with another human being, allowing them to completely be who they are. Connection is just non-conditionality with another person.

As I watched her slowly leave this earthly realm, her departure allowed love to arrive. Not just the kind of love you get at the end of a Rom Com movie but something full, all encompassing, something that has nothing to do with me, you or what's even happening. Love, to me, isn't just about feeling great; it's about allowing one's heart to stretch, encompassing the boundless potential of *all* experience. The sadness and grief I felt seemed to etch out new depth to experience love more, to let go and fall into grief fully, completely; to cry deeply, unashamedly. To do this without self-judgment, without fear of feeling, is ultimate human liberation.

As her physical form took its last breath, I felt very peaceful and I think she did too. The sunlight flooded through the hospice window and lit up the dust floating in the air. It was like thousands of fairies bursting with light. I held her hand and whispered: "It's ok to go mum, we are all fine, we will be fine; be at peace now, be at peace, my love; we all love you." As I whispered in her ear, she finally started to look at peace, the burden of holding on for her children released.

# *Reflection*

This is a wonderful story that illustrates how love, unencumbered by our personal thinking, helps us get through difficult times. We frequently think that there are certain situations, like death, that need to be sad and difficult. However, the power of love is what gets us through everything.

## Chapter 18

# The Magic of Living in Love

*Hope and faith go together. With hope and faith in your heart you will find the perfect path you seek.*

—SYDNEY BANKS

## Erika

If you look back on your life, you can see that life is always presenting you with the opportunity to realize a deeper truth, to see a bigger picture. We've all had light-bulb moments, maybe just a few that jump out at us over the course of our lives. Those moments change us. They bring us things like humility, forgiveness, relief or the ability to let go of something. They make us feel like we're ok, or life's ok in a way we'd never realized, which brings a level of reassurance and peace of mind that permeates the way we feel in a very profound way. It changes us from that point forward.

For me, many of those moments have happened in the realm of my relationships. I've had some of my most profound realizations specifically around my marriage, and the benefits seem to spill out into the rest of my life. Ironically, those moments of realization that made my life ultimately better usually started out as a source of tension or irritation for me. My understanding of the Principles is what gave me the grace and maturity to turn that around and take my relationship, and ultimately my life, down a very different path.

# *Reflection*

This is a great story that illustrates how new insights bring continual change and a deeper understanding of the Principles. As we go deeper, we are touched by more of our experiences in life rather than stressed by them. It feels like falling in love with life.

We have seen people go from feelings of anger and insecurity to feelings of love and compassion as their understanding deepens, sometimes within the same conversation. Each time we get an insight and our level of consciousness rises, we see a new relationship. So, if your life or your relationship doesn't look different, you're not going deeper and your level of consciousness will remain the same. There is so much beyond what we currently know about the possibilities for living in beautiful feelings. As you continue to go deeper into those feelings, you'll grow wiser and happier, and things will keep getting better and better.

## *Living From a Deeper Feeling of Love and Understanding*

We've noticed the following things about couples who live from following a deep understanding of the Principles. These characteristics are the natural result of a deep sense of love.

## Being in Service to Each Other

### John

John was an extremely stressed out owner of a small construction company. He felt that his wife, Yolanda, should take care of everything at home—the children and their farm. He was always so overwhelmed thinking about the details of his business, he didn't think he should have to be involved in anything else. He was blind to how his thinking made life appear easy for his wife and hard for him. Yolanda thought that she was having to manage everything, and John had it easy. All he had to do was get to work and come home, while she had to manage everything all the time. Additionally, when he came home from work, she had to take care of him, too. As the couple started to awaken to how the Principles worked and quieted down, they both began to see how to be helpful to each other. The household started to run more smoothly, and everything felt less stressful. One night Yolanda said, "I think you should help the boys with their homework this year." John immediately reacted, thinking that she should do it, but then he was able to see that he could just let that go and said, "Okay, I can try that." That one simple change was a huge revelation for John, who was able to see that his own thinking was creating his anger and keeping him from being in service to his family.

# Reflection

Hopefully you understand from what you have read so far that before people learned the Principles, they would often take things personally. When that happens they're not thinking about how to be more in service to their partners. As human beings we usually think about our own needs and desires. We get caught up in our own world instead of thinking of others and what would be helpful to them. You may have noticed this about yourself that when you get caught up in your thinking—it's all about *you*. We have heard from many of our clients that they were blindsided when their spouse asked for a divorce or simply moved out. The one who leaves often says they were neglected, and the one left behind often hadn't realized they were being neglectful until it was too late. If you were to have a closer look, you would see that self-absorbed thinking is the outcome of an insecure state of mind. Whereas thinking in terms of serving your partner to make things easier for him or her is a wonderful feeling.

It's so easy for couples to take one another for granted. Many of our couples have reported that one or the other had been complaining that they felt neglected, alone in the relationship or that they couldn't communicate. It was only after that person either filed for divorce or started an affair that the neglectful partner took notice. Unfortunately, by that time, people often believe that it's probably too late to save the marriage and often give up.

Just as you would tend to your garden by mowing, weeding and watering, you can tend to your partner with acts of kindness, for example, helping him or her with their chores or with their work when they are overwhelmed with a project or other task. The point is that you check in with your partner to see if they need help with anything, or if they just need a break, or a night out, perhaps. Then take them on an outing of their choosing, not yours! These are the things our clients do for one another, automatically, after they've been threatened with divorce. The trouble is that the one being tended to doesn't trust that the change is sincere and that it will last. We can't emphasize enough the value of truly listening to your partner, not to what you want them to say or what you think they are saying but actually to what they *are* saying. It's much simpler than you may think.

## Keeping a Connection

### Christine

When my husband, Sam, and I first started living together almost 32 years ago, we both wanted to live in the most positive feelings we could have for each other. We agreed that arguing was not something that either one of us wanted in our relationship. He had been through a difficult relationship with his first wife, and I was a marriage and family therapist who saw what negativity can do to couples and families. Plus, as a marriage and family therapist, I didn't think it was good for business for me to get divorced. So I warned him when we were getting married that we would not be getting divorced no matter what! [*laugh*]

Maintaining a positive attitude and coming from a good feeling became more important to us than being right, taking things personally or being in control. Now to be honest, I'm still really learning how to stay in that beautiful feeling and not let the stresses I create in my head contaminate that feeling. I'm continually shocked at how my thinking can trick me into being stressed, talking in a harsh tone and needing to be in control.

One of the things that I learned early on was that Sam was a really good barometer for my level of stress. I would be blind to how much thinking I was doing and how urgent things looked to me at times. Sam would react emotionally to me. As I observed these interactions, I realized that he was not tolerant of my busy mind and stressful feelings. I wasn't *making* him feel anything, but I could tell after a while that when I got stressed out, he would get reactive to me in small ways and sometimes in big ways. I realized that my job was to use his reaction as a signal that I was going too fast and needed to quiet down. When I did this, my feeling changed, and we would both get back to interacting from a positive feeling again.

For me, it's about keeping the feeling of love alive rather than letting it be a memory or concept. I can tell the difference in myself, when I think about how much I love my husband and I am filled with that beautiful feeling. It is real right then and there. When I'm not in touch with that feeling, I know intellectually that I love him, but I'm just not feeling it at the time! It is easy to have thoughts about the other person, especially if you've been with them for a long time. We frequently "go to sleep," so to speak, and don't realize that we're focusing on our own negative thoughts. I use irritation, bother and discontent as a signal that I need to get back to my wisdom and see what is going on with me. This is so helpful in righting the ship again. We both have little idiosyncrasies that we can focus on and react to, but neither one of us takes them seriously for long. Forgetting about past moments, when one of us gets into a bad place, is important. True forgiveness is when I forget all about those bad moments! My low moods still bring to mind everything Sam did when I was feeling insecure in the past. It all seems so real. Knowing that it is always a bad idea to go along with a negative feeling and a negative line of thinking saves me from being tricked into creating a reality I do not want to live in. So remembering that negativity is not something I want to focus on, and also remembering that positivity is always the way back helps me to protect my relationship from my own insecurities.

I've learned things about myself by living with my husband that I had no clue were part of my own thinking. Like teasing and talking down to someone who thought differently than I did. I remember one day, I made some comment to Sam, and he said, "Do you think that I'm stupid?" I was startled and thought to myself, *Oh, of course I don't think he's stupid,* and then I let my thinking go. Then he said the same thing a second time. That's when I knew I needed to take a look at what I was doing that would cause him to ask that question, since that was the furthest thing from my mind. As I observed myself, I realized that I frequently talked to him as if he were a child or not very bright! I had to chuckle because I remember my mother talking to my father in the same way. I got quiet about it, and I thought, *Ok, what do I need to do differently?* I realized that if I talked to Sam the same way that I talked to my best girlfriend, I'd be ok. I didn't have expectations or judgments of her! That realization caused a shift in me, and I guess I changed. He never asked me again if I thought he was stupid. I made adjustments in myself, instead of getting defensive or blaming him. I am doubtful that we would have such a wonderful relationship without our commitment to living in that feeling and being grateful that I had learned something about how the Principles work through us.

## *Reflection*

What's important to realize is that as you go along in your life, if your goal is to stay in a beautiful feeling with your spouse, you can find your way back even when you get temporarily distracted. When either one of you becomes distant and starts to focus on what you don't like, things may look bleak and hopeless. These are the times to take yourself by the hand and start to look out for the illusions you are caught up in. Listen to your wisdom so that you start to quiet down and wait for your state of mind to shift. We all get off course from time to time, but when you know that your ability to reconnect with your partner is on the inside then you know where to look. It is insidious how quickly a good relationship can go wrong or how distance happens when you start focusing on things outside of your relationship more than you focus on being present and sharing love.

We have found that being kind and being positive can never hurt. It is always insecurity that causes us to say things we don't really mean or take things personally and get our feelings hurt. Unfortunately, human beings are still in the process of learning how to be with each other without contaminating the relationship with our insecurities. Knowing this helps us to change and get through difficult times.

## Quieting Down

### Robert

Maine is a place where my mind has always seemed to naturally clear. I do things I love, and our home is in the trees and on the water. It is a serene and peaceful place, and I stop working. So it has been a great place to experiment with my understanding of the Principles, which I can see is helping me. I now understand why bow hunting for deer was always my favorite thing to do growing up. It was the only time I ever sat still and allowed my mind to be clear. Rarely do you ever get an animal close enough to shoot at. You just have to sit still and wait, doing nothing and listening for the slightest sounds. I felt peaceful.

My wife, Julie, kept asking me, "Are you ok; do you feel alright? What is that look on your face?" "What are you thinking about?" and I kept telling her, "I am trying to think about nothing; that is what is different." I think I had a happy, goofy look on my face, and she was not used to it. It was like I figured something out, or I was getting away with something.

# *Reflection*

Robert and Julie always got along better when they went away on vacation, but when they came back home all of their old thinking would return, and with it all of the stress and anger. They would soon be fighting again. Upon learning about the Principles, they were excited to see if they could maintain their vacation state of mind as they returned to home and work.

Most people do not understand that their stress is always coming from their state of mind. As people quiet down, their behavior improves automatically. People in quiet states of mind tend to be kinder, gentler, more considerate and more generous.

## Enrique

Enrique was a policeman in a large city. He worked as a patrolman in a particularly crime-laden section of the city. He started to become interested in the Principles and attended a talk by Sydney Banks. When he returned to work, he called to say, "Everyone is so slow." I laughed and said, "No, it's not that people slowed down; it's your mind that has quieted down." He didn't realize how much listening to Mr. Banks had impacted him. His mind quieted, and as a result, everything in the outside world looked slower.

# *Reflection*

It seems to many people as though they live in a fast-paced world, and they try to keep up with everything they see that needs to be done. It feels to them as though they're on a treadmill, and the world keeps increasing the speed.

The truth is that the treadmill only moves at the pace of our own thinking. When we're in a hurry, rushing around, we tend to be shorter tempered and impatient. We tend to blame people around us for the fact that we're in a hurry, and you know where that leads.... It's our busy-mindedness causing us to feel impatient, and so it feels as if the world is on fast forward.

When we slow down, we get our bearings back, and life doesn't appear to be so fast-paced. We feel in control rather than feeling controlled by the world and the people around us. As a result, we are automatically more pleasant to be around.

George Pransky tells the perfect story to illustrate this point. He describes a ride at an amusement park that is a cylinder hooked up to ropes and pulleys. As people walk through the cylinder, it begins turning. The faster you walk, the faster the cylinder goes, so people think they have to go fast in order to get out, but really the opposite is true. You have to walk slowly in order to get out. The faster you go, the harder it is to get out. The same is true in life. The trick is to do the opposite of what you think when you're insecure. Slowly, step by step, you can walk through the cylinder easily without feeling caught in it. It's a great analogy for people caught up in their own busy thinking as though it is their life making them feel stressed. They think they have to go faster to deal with their life.

## Be Kind and Loving

### Barbara and Alan

Barbara and Alan were caught up in negative thinking about each other. Try as they might to fix what was wrong in the other, nothing was changing. They were both convinced that there was little hope to save their marriage, but neither wanted a divorce. One day, Barbara went home to help care for her aging parents. Her mother was in her 80s and had been stricken with a chronic illness for much of her adult life. Her father was her mom's caregiver. What Barbara saw when she went home was how patient, calm, respectful and loving her parents were with each other. She realized that caring for her mother brought joy to her father because he could help the woman he had loved for years. It wasn't a burden; it was a joy. She was so touched by the feeling between them, and she wanted that feeling in her relationship with Alan.

# *Reflection*

People often think relationships are hard and have to be worked on. In fact, the reverse is true. Relationships actually improve the less people work on them. People work on what they think is the problem, trying to fix it so that they feel in love again. We've all been conditioned to solve problems so we can feel better, but that's "putting the cart before the horse." When people look for a positive feeling within, problems disappear and solutions appear instead. When people are in positive feeling states, their tendency is to nurture the relationship, see the humor in things and see each other's innocence.

> *Be kind whenever possible. It is always possible.*
> —DALAI LAMA

This is a wonderful quote, worth taking a few moments to reflect on. Even when someone is not behaving kindly toward you, if you can see that their bad behavior is the result of their distorted thinking, you'll no doubt feel compassion for them. Your compassion and understanding might even help the person who is out of sorts. At the very least, you won't make it any worse. Loving kindness will grow your relationship like fertilizer grows gardens, and it's absolutely free. So dive in and pay attention to the feeling you're coming from rather than focusing on trying to solve problems. It's easy to find a nice feeling when you take your mind off your personal thinking.

## Lighten Up and Let Things Go

### Christine

My husband and I were moving into our first house, and as the furniture came in, I was asked where things would go. I told Sam, "Let's put the green sofa in the big living room." He said, "What green sofa?" I said, "Ha ha, the only sofa we have." We were pretty poor back then, so we definitely had only one sofa. He said, "It is not green, it's brown." I thought he was making fun, and I laughed again. He started getting louder and said, "Are you playing games on me?" I realized that he was serious about it being brown, and he thought I was messing with his head! So I got quiet and thought about it. I remembered that sometimes brown fabric turned green with the sea air. I went over and pulled the cushions out; sure enough, where the air couldn't reach the material, it was brown. So now, I think, *Ok, so he is seeing this sofa through his memory, and I am seeing it as it is now, green. Anyone who looks at it, who has never seen it before will surely think the sofa is green.*

When our first visitor came to the house, I took them over to the sofa and asked them what color it was. They said, "BROWN!!" I nearly died! I really thought everyone would see it as green! For months, I quizzed everyone who came to the house, and nearly everyone saw it as brown. Only two other people thought it was green. This disagreement could have escalated into a fight, but instead it became a humorous game.

## *Reflection*

It's wonderfully freeing when we don't take ourselves or each other too seriously. We're more lighthearted, and we tend to be more humorous, which helps to lighten the mood of the moment. When we're in a more lighthearted state of mind, we can get curious and even laugh at how we see a different reality. In other words, we're more objective about things, and that's very freeing and can even feel empowering.

## Helen and Sid

Helen and Sid were married with four children. Sid worked in the hotel that they lived in. One night Helen called Sid in for dinner, and with all four children sitting around the table she served dinner and then sat down at the other end of the table from her husband. Suddenly, she looked at Sid and said, "That's it! I know what you're thinking." Then she slammed her fork down on the table, got up and marched to her room. Sid looked at his children and said, "What did I do now?" Everyone looked at each other as if to say, "What was that about?"

# Reflection

Frequently we feel angry about what we believe other people are thinking. We never really know what someone else is thinking; we're just making it up. Even if the other person was harboring negative thoughts about us, it's still our judgmental thinking of what they did or the situation that is upsetting to us.

One of the reasons there is a marriage and family therapy profession is because people are not very good at talking to each other and really listening. Of course, this is never a problem when you're just falling in love. It seems like you can talk about anything and everything. Sometimes, after you've lived with someone for a while, you start to think they should know what you want. So when they don't, you might take it personally and blame them for being inadequate as a partner, or you may think that they are purposely trying to make you feel bad. No matter how long you've been with someone, it's wise to be open about what you want. No one can read your mind. Also, we change our minds frequently, so how can we expect our partner to keep up with us? We are always amazed at how little couples really know about each other when they come to us for help.

## Chapter 19

# Keeping the Magic Alive for Life

*When a lost couple finds wisdom and understanding*
*within their own consciousness, their marital problems will*
*start to dissipate.*

–Sydney Banks

## Jane and Tom

**Jane:** Tom and I had been in an on-and-off relationship for about three and a half years. It was one of those argumentative relationships. We were miserable much of the time. We'd split apart, but something kept bringing us back together. I just really wanted to have that close, beautiful, soul-sharing relationship we had when we first got together. But we couldn't quite get there. We were both searching for peace, looking for a spiritual answer. I was meditating and doing yoga every day. We both had a lot of beliefs about everything. One strong belief was that society was all messed up, and that was why it was so hard to feel peaceful. So we just kept moving farther and farther away from society until we wound up living up in the Yukon, in the wilderness. It was just the two of us in this little cabin at the end of a 90-mile-long lake. We had no electricity and no running water; we were really off the grid.

We had a lot of adventures there; it was a beautiful place, but we'd still argue and bicker. Then we went to visit friends in Vancouver, and I wound up hearing a cassette tape of Syd Banks. As I listened to the tape, I started having this beautiful, peaceful feeling.

Soon afterward I ended up going to Salt Spring Island where I met Syd and his wife, Barb. I went to one of Syd's talks. The feeling in the room, and seeing all these couples who were happy together, gave me such hope. I just couldn't believe I was seeing all these people in happy relationships. [*laughs*] Something I really wanted deep in my heart but had given up on ever finding.

When Syd started talking, I wasn't really understanding what he was saying, but the feeling was so strong, it honestly didn't matter that I wasn't understanding it. At one point he said something about Divine Consciousness being within each one of us. At that moment, my world changed.

I had thought that finding peace and happiness required some sort of search, but when Syd said that and I got that insight, I felt this joy and incredible peace. I just knew that my happiness came from within me and not from outside of me. That was the insight that really changed everything.

I went back home to the Yukon. It was so funny because when I went back, all the little things that used to bother me just didn't bother me anymore. Before, every time I got in a bad mood or felt down, it was Tom's fault. [*laughs*] I didn't know any better. [*laughs*] I just thought if I'm sad, that means he's doing something (or not doing something) to make me feel that way; or if I'm annoyed, then he's doing something to make me feel annoyed. [*laughs*] This time, I wasn't feeling unhappy; I wasn't feeling sad. I felt so at peace. I felt like I had found what I had been searching for. And also, you know, if any little thought would come up, I knew it was just my thought; it was just me. It wasn't anything else, and it was easier to just let it go then. It was unbelievable.

**Tom:** When Jane came back, I noticed she was a lot easier to get along with. [*laughs*]

As Jane said, we were living in a very remote place that was 60 miles from the nearest tiny, tiny little town, at the end of a lake with no roads and no way to get there except by boat. Jane ended up having to go back into this little town because she needed medical treatment. Before leaving, she said to me, "I will see you in a couple of weeks." But she didn't come back in a couple of weeks, she actually came back a month later; and during that time, winter arrived and the lake froze over. I spent an entire month completely by myself with no one to talk to, nothing. Something really hit me during that time. I was alone and realized that all the things that seemed to be making me miserable were no longer there, but I was still miserable. It hit me that everything I was trying to get away from I brought with me in my head. It was as if I hadn't gotten away from anything. I still wasn't happy!

**Jane:** Prior to hearing Syd, Tom and I couldn't imagine being married and bringing children into the world. I couldn't imagine being in a relationship stable enough to bring up children.

Things really changed after that trip to Salt Spring. So many limiting beliefs fell away. We moved from the Yukon to the island, and within three months, we decided to get married. Both of us knew it was the right thing to do; we told our parents, and they were overjoyed. On New Year's Day 1977, we had our wedding in my sister's finished basement that she had decorated beautifully. Soon we had our daughter, and then, three and a half years later had our son. It was that beautiful foundation that was the saving grace for our marriage and for raising our children. Not that there weren't ups and downs; there definitely were. [*laughs*] You know, large and small, but just knowing that the answer is within made all the difference. We also knew that both of us, and our children, had wisdom and health within us that we could turn to, to get through the hard times. It helped us go through those ups and downs with a lot more grace and sanity. We are still learning how to live life gracefully from an understanding of the Three Principles. It's always unfolding more deeply.

There have been times in our marriage when we felt quite distant from each other and yet, you know, there was that knowing, underneath it, that it's just Thought; it's not what's real. What is true is that love is what we really are. That wisdom comes to the surface as we encounter things that seem negative, and we come out with a deeper understanding. I'm so grateful, and seriously, it's never ending. It continues to happen to us.

**Tom:** We have been married for 40 years; we have two incredible kids who are our best friends, and we have three grandchildren with one more coming in September. None of this would have been in my life if I hadn't somehow stumbled across Syd and his teachings. I mean, I can't convey what a beautiful thing that is—a life I almost missed. I just thank the Lord, or whatever you want to call it, that somehow we were fortunate enough to stumble across this when we did. I even wonder if I would still be here the way I was living; it was pretty risky. [*laughs*]

## *Reflection*

You can see that Jane and Tom were doing the best they could to live in a stress-free, positive feeling, but because they didn't know about the Principles they thought the stress was coming from the outside world. So they tried a geographical cure, thinking they had to get far away from society in order to feel less stress. This is not an unusual reaction. Many people seek to change things in the outside world to find greater happiness, i.e. a new job, a new house, a different partner. However, after they changed their external reality, they realized that they were just as stressed and unhappy as before. Deep down inside they knew they could be happy. They just hadn't found the answer, but since they were looking to feel better they were open to finding out about something deeper. This is an example of how wisdom operates even when we don't know it is.

When Jane and Tom began to learn about the Principles, they realized they couldn't run away from their stress because they were creating it. When they both awakened to the nature of Thought, their life changed across the board, and they got what they were looking for without doing anything. The change simply came from awakening to the Principles.

Needless to say, seeing that they didn't have to get away from society, they were able to create a life that was much easier and simpler. It didn't stop there; however, throughout the next forty years, they continued to find a nicer state of mind, returning to their wisdom to help them navigate the ups and downs of life.

## Sara

I was in a relationship with Luke, who lived several hundred miles away. We tried to make a long-distance relationship work, but he couldn't maintain a monogamous relationship being so far away from me. Luke told me that he met and slept with another woman. He said it was too hard to maintain a long-distance relationship and that he was going to continue to see this woman and any others he wanted. I was heartbroken for a while but decided that I really had loved him as a person as well as a partner. After a month or so, I contacted him to just say hi. I was happy to talk with him and catch up. Luke was with another woman by that time, and she had moved in with him. That hurt, but I figured that, if the only way to keep him in my life was as a friend, I would have to do that. I called a month or so later, and they were about to part ways as well. I invited him to travel to my town to de-stress from the situation. I really did not know what was going to happen, but I knew that I really cared about him and wanted him to be happy, if not with me, then with someone else. As it turned out, we had a wonderful reunion, and he asked me to come to live in his town. I have been here for six years now, and we are a very happy couple. I run into the women he was with from time to time in our small town and have been friendly to them. Knowing what I know about the Principles, it is not hard to find empathy in my heart for these women. After all, Luke's a pretty good guy! And if I am being true to myself, I have to drop any jealousy, second-guessing or fears with him, or the relationship won't work.

Understanding that Luke was doing the best he could see to do during all of our time together—good and bad times—was a true gift. And knowing that what happened in the past can't be changed really helped me. Otherwise my thoughts would have tortured me, and eaten away at my happiness. Recognizing this helped me put the past aside, truly forgive and forget, and move on. If I didn't know about thought and how it tricks you into believing that it is real, I would be living a completely different life now. I am very grateful and totally in love with this man.

# *Reflection*

Sara let love guide her instead of listening to her insecure thinking. Here is a clue that will help you understand the simplicity of coming from love: See innocence in yourself as well as in your partner. Our ability to come from love isn't affected by the situations of our life. When we come from love, it helps us to get through whatever challenges we're enduring (vis à vis our thinking) in the moment.

## Marika

Our story began when Richard and I were very young and got married in 1975. Our mantra in those days was, "Won't it be great when…we finish school, find a good job, get married, get a house," in other words, putting off gratitude and contentment for some future event.

Soon I was not feeling the happiness I expected. On the outside, we appeared accomplished, both with good jobs, enjoying our hobbies and we had a deep commitment to one another. Yet after almost a year of marriage, I was feeling sad, thinking, "Is this it?" Throughout my teens and college, I had been a searcher for answers, via religion, books and the then popular group therapy/sensitivity sessions. I embraced the philosophy of the day: "Make love, not war," but somehow I sensed I was missing something.

I noticed a little poster inviting people to a weekly meeting to listen to tapes by Sydney Banks. We had read a bit about the man and what he was sharing, and we were intrigued. We walked into our hosts' lovely home and were warmly greeted and welcomed to join in to listen to a tape.

As I listened, I felt an inner stirring and a recognition as I let the words wash over me, and at the same time, my mind was scrambling to make sense of it all. The people in the room radiated happiness that I, at first, judged as phony. But by the end of the evening I sensed that they had found the contentment that I was searching for. Something inside me had woken up. I couldn't understand it, but I liked the feeling I was experiencing. The words I heard seemed so simple, yet the feeling was so deep. Richard had a nice feeling about the evening too, so we now had something new and meaningful to share.

A short time later, we had the good fortune of meeting Syd and were profoundly struck by his genuine caring and his powerful loving presence. We walked away from that first meeting feeling as if we were in a dream after we had only discussed what I thought were ordinary daily matters. We understood little at the beginning but were drawn by the quality of feeling and deeper sense of love of life than we had ever experienced before.

By simply listening to spiritual facts, we noticed a deep shift in what we experienced in life, in our work, but mostly in finding satisfaction and happiness in daily life with one another. Unlike previous learning, there was nothing to do. It was the opposite, quieting my thinking to allow my fresh insights to guide me. I no longer viewed my life and relationships so seriously, blaming events for my feelings. We began to understand that our happiness is within. Sydney never told us what to do, but we learned from his example in simple daily living. We were touched by the simple love and kindness he showed to his then wife, his two children and his mother-in-law who lived with them. I observed how Syd and Barb listened to and respected one another, sharing a deep connection. This was so helpful to us in the early years of our lives together. We witnessed and experienced for ourselves, the happiness that was possible in being ordinary. We could see how going about our work, caring for our home and being together could be magical and fulfilling. I had never seen or experienced such connection to life.

Over our 45 years together, we have also faced some challenges together as we held differences in thought about various things. We find comfort in momentarily setting our issues aside. We give ourselves a chance to let something new re-awaken from within. Time and time again, we are reassured and reminded of our true nature, our spiritual essence and that we innocently or knowingly are creators of our experience via the thoughts we choose to pay attention to. I've found it helpful to step away from a feeling we don't like between us and look inside to regain a feeling of love and appreciation for life, and it does wonders when we come together again. One thing I seem to keep learning is letting go, being open and seeing what comes. What always brings us back together is our common understanding, the glimmer that the Three Principles of Mind, Consciousness and Thought create all our experiences and feelings, and we are the result of these Principles in action. It is the foundation of our relationship that we keep coming back to. Resting in that knowledge brings us peace. It also tells us that if we don't like what we are seeing, it is just a thought, a temporary creation. I remember Syd telling me, "Look for a feeling!" At times when I can't see my way out of a situation, those words come back to me, and give me solace. I learned that when I rest in my positive feelings, it comes with helpful information on what to do next and how to respond to a challenge.

Although we have our ups and downs, I am feeling more gentleness and appreciation for Richard. I'm listening more for his wisdom as we navigate life together. My compassion for him is growing as I see him creating his world, just as I am. As a result, I am also feeling the same compassion coming back from him as I face my challenges. This helps bring about a feeling of forgiveness and closeness. I'm also gaining a sense of Divine Mind at play, providing opportunities for us to look inside and to grow.

On a practical level, since both of us lead full lives with work, family, hobbies and caring for our home, we have found value in taking time for shared experiences in doing what we love together. Some of the things we enjoy are going for a walk nearby, watching a sunset, a canoe paddle, enjoying family, playing with our grandchildren or simply doing nothing, all of which are ways we've chosen to experience harmony together. However, it's not necessarily "the doing," but finding that resting space within ourselves and together that allows insights and beautiful feelings to come forth. This is when we are at our best, acknowledging the loving feelings that bubble up from inside. And sometimes I take a pause on my own to quiet my busy thoughts, honoring that divine space within. Then I see it more in every other person I encounter. We are all the same.

I have a feeling that we would not be together nor have experienced so many wonderful things together had we not had that nudge, in our early days, toward understanding that our love and happiness come from within before we see it in the world. I love getting the glimpses of our connection to all. When I see Richard playing with our grandchildren, I see a new sweetness in his face, and I fall in love all over again. Perhaps this is an example of living in love that we'd always hoped for. We are forever grateful to have been woken up to the wisdom Syd shared with us and for the lives we have been given.

## *Reflection*

Marika and her husband, Richard, didn't have big problems, but they knew there was still something missing. They realized that it wasn't about their situation or circumstance because no matter how much they accomplished, they still felt something was missing. As their inner world changed, they found a new level of contentment, positivity and enjoyment in their lives. They began to see the power of living in love. After forty-five years, you can still feel the love, respect and understanding that they have for one another.

### Bob and Christa

**Bob:** Christa and I met in our senior year of high school. We became really close friends for a number of years. After high school we both chose different paths but ran into each other regularly.

One warm summer evening in 1975, I had a conversation with my neighbor, Chip Chipman. I had no idea at the time that this conversation would change my life. Chip and Jan had just recently met Sydney Banks and said he was an enlightened man. As Chip was telling me about what he was learning, I got goosebumps. I decided at that point to seek out this "enlightened man" despite some skepticism on my part.

As chance would have it, Syd gave his first public talk on Salt Spring Island a few weeks later. As I had been a spiritual searcher for many years, looking for answers to age-old questions, I decided to travel to Salt Spring Island to hear him speak for the first time. I could not say that I understood all he was saying, but it resonated as truth in my soul. Some of the things Syd said that night were familiar from my years of seeking truth. I saw many of the pieces fit together from all I had learned and experienced. That was comforting. What was unique was that this time I came away with a powerful, deep knowing, a feeling that I can only describe as one of calm elation.

I woke up the next morning with that same feeling. The world looked different. It was the same world, just brighter, more optimistic. I was seeing the world from a new, elevated perspective. My thoughts were creating my world! My life of searching ended the night I heard Sydney Banks. There was nothing to figure out; to me this was the ultimate answer. It just felt right. I saw that all the problems of the world were created by fear, and fear is just another thought created from an insecure state of mind. I was convinced that the entire planet was going to change within the next few months or years (I was very young.) I envisioned the possibility of a world living in peace and harmony.

I couldn't wait to share this incredible experience with Christa. I told her that I heard an enlightened man, and it changed everything. We talked and talked, and eventually I convinced her to come and hear Syd speak.

It was then that I began to realize that Christa was more than just a friend. She was the person I thought about all the time, who I visited every holiday when we were home, the person I missed when she went to Europe. Finally, it dawned on me: Here was the perfect person for me. I loved her, and she was my closest friend.

So "out of the blue," I asked her to marry me. [*laughs*] We basically started our romantic relationship because of the new understanding Sydney Banks shared with us. It absolutely changed everything. We have been married for many years, still going strong. We love each other, we love being with each other and we have a lot of fun together. Lots of laughs! We are completely different people in terms of the way we see things and the way we do things. But that doesn't matter. It's not about our personal thinking. We work together for our relationship and for our family. Anyway, after forty years... First, we had a strong friendship, which brought us together, but it is the feeling of love and caring for each other that keeps us together and growing as a couple. There have been many ups and downs in our life, but all we ever need to do is remember: It's just Thought, and the ship rights itself. Every time.

**Christa:** When I got back home from a time studying in Europe, I visited Bob in the Gulf Islands. Over that past year, we had gone in different directions. So when I left my visit with Bob, I clearly remember thinking on my ferry ride back…well that's the end of that. And thought I would never see him again, to be honest, because we had gone in such different ways. [*laughs*] So I was very surprised that he came to see me that fall.

I had just started back at university, and Bob came for a visit and said, "Well I found the secret to life!" It started out with Bob saying some crazy things, like this table isn't real, it's just thought. I was arguing with him, but I could not deny that there was an incredible new feeling emanating from him. It was a sense of calm, yet vital and alive at the same time.

He was elated; he heard Syd Banks say, "happiness comes from within," and that "thought creates reality." It turned into philosophical discussions exploring the facts like young people do. The outcome is that I felt fantastic, and all of a sudden, here's my best friend again, and we were having these wonderful talks. Bob left town after a few days, but that feeling stayed with me. Reflecting back, what happened because of that understanding and the feeling that came with it, my intellect calmed down and I began to experience more happiness, so I no longer tried to control everything with my intellect. My search stopped; I knew Bob had found the truth, as discovered and taught by Sydney Banks, and the truth is found inside each one of us.

And as Bob says, he invited me to one of Syd's talks. Syd was so powerful; you hear yourself when you listen to him. All the important things I learned as a child, all the beautiful things, suddenly came alive. And that changed me; I started to see this feeling of love as knowledge and wisdom.

In '77 we got married and settled into our lives as an ordinary young married couple. As Bob said, because our marriage started with this understanding, it has truly been amazing. We are grateful and know we've been very fortunate. We know that unconditional love is always our number one focus. As Bob said, we are different; we have different opinions and all of that stuff. But that doesn't matter; what matters is living in the feeling of unconditional love. That is still alive and keeps growing in us and in our lives…and here we are forty years later, still learning and living an incredible life.

## *Reflection*

This story illustrates what is possible. It shows that the power of understanding doesn't come from anyone other than ourselves. Sydney Banks never told this couple what to do. Their behaviors were the result of their new understanding, and they created a beautiful life as a result.

> *All you have to do is point yourself in the general direction and then do nothing.*
>
> —Sydney Banks

# *Final Reflection*

It is our hope that we have given you enough stories and guidance to help you point yourself in the direction of your own spiritual nature. Looking within and letting a deeper feeling of peace, serenity and assurance come through you will have a magical effect on all of your relationships. There is nothing you have to do to make anything happen other than look within yourself and be open to see how the Principles work within you to constantly and consistently bring you an experience of life. And since understanding these Principles can have such a transformative effect on you and the people you interact with, just imagine what it could do for the rest of the world.

We wrote this book to help people live in greater peace and harmony. Sydney Banks found the key to the mystery of life. The Three Principles are always at work, creating reality for each of us. As more and more people come to understand the inner workings of the Principles, the world will improve as the level of consciousness rises. It was Sydney Banks' lifelong dream that understanding of the Principles would spread throughout the world to relieve all of the suffering. It is an honor for us to try to help make that dream a reality. If you have seen something in this book that helped you to live in love, please pass it along to others and then you will be part of the change.

There are now many ways to continue your learning journey. We have found that the deeper we continue to go into this beautiful way of seeing life and love, the more magical life appears. We hope it will be the same for you. Remember it's always about the feeling of love. *The Secret of Love* is that it is always inside of you.

> *Delving into the Three Principles is endless.*
>
> –Sydney Banks

We want to thank everyone for your stories and your enthusiasm in bringing this to life.

# Acknowledgments

We have found that when people are able to quiet down and listen, they have insights that help them go deeper into a feeling of love. If you liked this book and you'd like to go deeper, join us for our retreats and intensives designed for families and couples.

Authors' Websites
Lori: www.3principlestherapy.com/
Christine: www.hcechawaii.com/

The following are websites of contributors that are also excellent resources:
www.sydbanks.com
www.3PGC.org
www.sydneybanks.org/
www.threeprinciplesfoundation.org/
www.threeprinciplesmovies.com/

Websites and email addresses of practitioners who contributed stories and quotes:
Brooke: www.cypressinitiative.org; www.sparkcurriculum.org
Chip and Jan: www.vantageconsult.com
Christa: ed-talks.com
Dicken: www.3principlesmentoring.com
Elsie: www.3phd.net/
Erika: www.pranskyandassociates.com/
Helen Neal-Ali: www.cypressinitiative.org; www.lcclearningcenter.org
George Pransky: PranskyandAssociates.com
Jack: www.healthrealize.com/
Joe Boyle: J2DBoyle@gmail.com
Judy: www.three-principles.com/
Kara: www.pranskyandassociates.com/
Keith: keithblevens@gmail.com
Mark: www.drmarkhoward.com/
Rudi Kennard: www.3pmovies.com; www.innatewellbeing.co.uk;
    www.innateevolution.com
Richard and Marika: rjmayer@telus.net
Tom: www.reflectionscounseling.com/; aa5216@wayne.edu

# About The Authors

## Lori Carpenos, LMFT

I was always fascinated by relationships, even as far back as childhood I remember observing my parents, their friends and my extended family. I wondered why some relationships were short lived, while others lasted a lifetime. I wondered why some relationships appeared to be full of contempt, while others were warm and loving. I wondered if it was a matter of finding the right person, some magical skill that some people possessed, or just plain luck.

Despite my innate curiosity about relationships, my parents encouraged me to study art education in college. After graduation and sending out 100 applications, I landed a great job teaching art in a middle school outside of Boston, Massachusetts. I was kept busy for three years while I simultaneously obtained an MEd with a concentration in art therapy. At twenty-five, I received tenure;

my parents thought I was golden. Nonetheless, I gave my notice at the end of the school year. Master's degree in hand, I packed my car with whatever I thought I'd need to drive 3500 miles solo to San Francisco, where I was certain art therapists were in high demand. My parents thought I was crazy, but they also knew they couldn't stop me.

Looking back, I now think my teaching career was replaced by a life calling to help people feel better about themselves and their lives. It began with trying to feel better about myself. I attended four years of weekly psychoanalysis at the Jungian Institute in San Francisco. Though I saw little improvement in my mood, I would have kept going had I not been coerced into attending a seminar by some well-meaning friends (a bunch of self-help junkies in search of the holy grail of happiness). The joke we shared was that everyone in San Francisco was either in therapy, a therapist or both, with most of us in the latter category. But who was this Sydney Banks I was about to listen to? I'd never heard of him. He wasn't a psychologist. In fact, there were no initials after his name (indicating an advanced degree). I went, assuming I was attending yet another personal growth lecture as part of the never-ending quest for self-improvement; none of which ever seemed to help me much.

I was completely caught off guard by what happened during that seminar. It was unimaginable. I began crying uncontrollably halfway through the talk, right up until the end. I'd always been someone who'd had control of her emotions. I was so embarrassed; I tried to hide it as best I could from my colleagues. Luckily, I was seated in the front row, so I thought my tears were well hidden, except perhaps for my shaking shoulders. It felt like a floodgate had opened. My emotions poured out against my will. All I could think was, *Why is this happening*? At the same time, I felt enormous relief—like discovering someone close to me was not going to die after all (but no one close to me was in any danger of dying at that time)! For some unknown reason I felt as though the weight of the world had been lifted, and I was going to be okay. I didn't even realize before then that I'd just been enduring life. Rather, I thought I was living life and that life was difficult for everyone, not just me. My life hadn't changed, but the feelings I walked around with had definitely shifted. I felt happier and lighter than I could ever remember. I gradually became more outgoing, more carefree and even funnier, as time went by. This all happened naturally, purely from gaining an understanding of how we all operate psychologically.

It was only years later that I realized that Syd Banks' explanation of the Three Principles had been the missing link in my understanding of life and love. The Principles provided the key that unlocked the magic I grew to understand was deep inside of me and everyone else.

I felt compelled to share what I had stumbled upon. I committed myself to the necessary coursework beyond my master's degree and two more years of internship hours to become a licensed marriage and family therapist. I wanted to help others discover the same understanding that had transformed my thinking. I was driven to learn as much as I could. The more my own state of mind improved, the more it fueled my personal mission to help others.

I opened a full-time private practice in 1994 centered upon teaching the Three Principles. Since then I've been honored to hear people's life stories. The personal stories are extraordinarily diverse, but what we all have in common is that we operate the same psychologically, regardless of our background or our current circumstances.

I can't imagine doing anything else now. It never feels like work. I learn as much from my clients as they learn from me, through the miracle of insight, as we reflect together on the role of the Principles in our lives.

Prior to starting my private practice, I worked in many settings including mental health agencies, hospitals and schools. About ten years ago I started documenting the stories I heard because some of the transformations I saw among my clients were so remarkable I felt I needed to write about them to help other people beyond my practice. When I realized I had enough stories to fill a book, I knew I needed help in writing that book. Luckily, Chris Heath came to mind first. Chris and I met in Coral Gables, Florida, in 1985, at the only training program available at the time that was based on Syd Banks' work.

It's a wonderful blessing to help my clients nurture, cultivate and honor the love they have for one another despite whatever personal difficulties they are experiencing. They show me the amazing gift of love two people can share in an intimate relationship. When you can truly appreciate the gift of an intimate relationship, you'll value what you have and take extraordinary care of it. I now know that the capacity for love lies within each of us.

## Christine Heath, LMFT, CSAC, MAC

I always had a dream that I could help make the world a better place, help people be happy and overcome adversity. I started out my career in the '70s as a consultant to programs for people with developmental and intellectual challenges. These were programs that helped to transition people who had been warehoused in state institutions and seen as throw-aways to people living in the community, learning and loving. I saw the potential and witnessed an awakening in people that no one thought possible. I was next drawn to the field of alcohol and drug addictions and soon I decided I wanted to be a family therapist. It seemed to me that this field had the best attitude toward people. It looked at people as healthy if their external systems were healthy. The problem is that no one ever told me what "health" looked like, and it seemed as if we had to address what was wrong with the individuals and families to help them get better. I was working with some of the most dysfunctional families on earth: violence and sexual abuse, addictions and more. I really tried to help people, but after about six years I realized that I was becoming more angry, depressed and anxious. I also realized that my clients would get better but they were still not happy and would frequently return to therapy after "graduating." I decided that I would get out of the therapy world and work in business because what I was doing wasn't making my clients happy, and I definitely wasn't happy!

I was also looking for a husband and decided that I should perhaps start looking in psychology conferences and workshops rather than bars and parties if I wanted to find someone who was healthy. There was a workshop coming to Minnesota with Dr. Roger Mills that was introducing a new paradigm in psychology based on the teachings of Sydney Banks. At the workshop, I had a profound shift that awakened me to the nature of life. I knew I would be teaching these Principles for the rest of my life. Before that weekend, my work was very focused on pathology and illness, so just the idea of being positive was revolutionary. I changed so much overnight that people thought I had joined the "Moonies," was on drugs or met a man! I was smiling so much my cheeks hurt, and I was no longer so serious or angry. My therapy immediately changed, and my chronic stress disappeared. I was happy!!

I immediately signed up for a training program in Miami where I met Sydney Banks. He was the most ordinary, extraordinary person I had ever met. He asked if he could help me. Of course, I said, yes! That became the beginning of my wild life in the world of the Three Principles. He was always there to listen to me. He would gently, and sometimes not so gently, guide me toward getting a deeper understanding of the Principles. Each day of my life I am reminded of the gifts I receive from this man. I wish Syd were alive today to see what has happened in the world.

I completed a yearlong training with Joe Bailey, LP, at the Advanced Human Studies Institute and set up one of the first outpatient clinics in the world founded on the Three Principles. Eventually, I settled in Hawaii and started another clinic, the Hawaii Counseling and Education Center. The Center has been providing services to the people of Hawaii for more than thirty-two years.

We developed programs for parents, teachers and students with educational challenges because of their mental health issues, provided counseling to incarcerated adults and youth, developed juvenile prevention and justice programs, adolescent and adult anger management/domestic violence programs, substance abuse treatment programs for adolescents and adults and general mental health counseling for children, adolescents, adults, families and couples. All of these programs are based on our best understanding of the Principles and have been successful in helping clients. We now have offices in four communities in Hawaii on two islands, Oahu and Hawaii. We continue to love our work and share what we know about the Principles with anyone who will listen!

I finally did find the man of my dreams, Sam Po'omaihealani at a racquetball club in Hawai'i. I have been living with Sam for thirty-two years and married twenty-seven years to this beautiful Hawaiian man who loves me more than any human being in the world has ever loved me. He has provided me with unwavering support that allowed me to continue my work and have a comfortable life. We have the home of our dreams with four unique and wonderful dogs (Polar Bear, Rhain, Ginger and Jake) and six cows!!

I have great friends and coworkers, most of whom are involved in this work in some way. I really can't think of anything else I could personally want for in this life. I feel lucky because after all these years, I am still just as jazzed about the power of this work, and I feel so grateful to have fallen in love with life. I am so grateful that I was able to become one of Syd's students. It was the greatest thing that has ever happened to me. I am forever grateful to him for helping not only me but the entire world.

*In this wonderful and inspiring book, the authors have presented
a Principle-based understanding of the true nature of the basis for
love, joy and ease in all relationships, augmented by a beautiful
collection of first-hand accounts, awakening the undeniable hope
that all relationships, despite any past difficulties and missteps,
have the ability to return home to this place of "mystery and
magic." The incremental insights into the Nature of the Three
Universal Principles of Mind, Consciousness and Thought
I have experienced over the last 34 years have improved and
often transformed every relationship in my life from those filled
with recurrent and significant struggle and conflict to those replete
with ease and an ability to share and receive love I could before
only have imagined.*

*This book is a must-read for all and one to share with any young
person you know as they enter the sometimes daunting world of
love and intimacy.*

–WILLIAM (BILL) PETTIT JR. MD, PSYCHIATRIST